Chan
Spa
Grammar

C000205386

Chambers

CHAMBERS

An imprint of Chambers Harrap Publishers Ltd
7 Hopetoun Crescent, Edinburgh, EH7 4AY

Chambers Harrap is an Hachette UK company

© Chambers Harrap Publishers Ltd 2009

Chambers® is a registered trademark of Chambers Harrap Publishers Ltd

This third edition published by Chambers Harrap Publishers Ltd 2009
First published as *Harrap's Spanish Grammar* in 1992
Second edition published 2003

The moral rights of the author have been asserted
Database right Chambers Harrap Publishers Ltd (makers)

All rights reserved. No part of this publication may be reproduced, stored in a
retrieval system, or transmitted in any form or by any means, electronic, mechanical,
photocopying, recording or otherwise, without the prior permission in writing of
Chambers Harrap Publishers Ltd, or as expressly permitted by law, or under terms
agreed with the appropriate reprographics rights organization. Enquiries concerning
reproduction outside the scope of the above should be sent to the Rights Department,
Chambers Harrap Publishers Ltd, at the address above.

You must not circulate this book in any other binding or cover and you must impose
this same condition on any acquirer.

A CIP catalogue record for this book is available from the British Library.

ISBN 978 0550 10512 7

10 9 8 7 6 5 4 3 2 1

We have made every effort to mark as such all words which we believe to be
trademarks. We should also like to make it clear that the presence of a word in the
book, whether marked or unmarked, in no way affects its legal status as a
trademark.

Every reasonable effort has been made by the author and the publishers to trace the
copyright holders of material quoted in this book. Any errors or omissions should be
notified in writing to the publishers, who will endeavour to rectify the situation for
any reprints and future editions.

Project Editors: Alex Hepworth, Kate Nicholson
With Helen Bleck

www.chambers.co.uk

Designed by Chambers Harrap Publishers Ltd, Edinburgh
Typeset in Rotis Serif and Meta Plus by Macmillan Publishing Solutions
Printed and bound in Spain by Graphy Cems

INTRODUCTION

This Spanish grammar from Chambers has been written to meet
the needs of all students of Spanish, and is particularly useful for
those taking school examinations. The essential rules of the Spanish
language have been explained in terms that are as accessible as
possible to all users. Where technical terms have been used then full
explanations of these terms have also been supplied. There is also
a full glossary of grammatical terminology on pages 11-18. While
literary aspects of the Spanish language have not been ignored, the
emphasis has been placed squarely on modern spoken Spanish. This
grammar, with its wealth of lively and typical illustrations of usage
taken from the present-day language, is the ideal study tool for all
levels – from the beginner who is starting to come to grips with
the Spanish language through to the advanced user who requires a
comprehensive and readily accessible work of reference.

This new edition boasts a smart new two-colour design to make
consultation even easier and more enjoyable.

PREFACE

This grammar is divided into two main sections:

Part I, THE FUNCTIONS OF SPANISH, explains how to use Spanish to refer to things and actions, to express conditions, emotions and the like. This list of functions does not claim to be exhaustive, but it does contain those most likely to cause difficulties for the English-speaking learner.

Part II, THE FORMS OF SPANISH, explains the formation of all the principal elements of the language. Here you can check the formation of tenses *etc*, or any unknown form you may come across in your reading.

A considerable effort has been made to explain not only *how* Spanish operates in different contexts, but, more importantly, to explain *why* it operates the way it does. This is an essential aspect of the book, because experience shows that what the learner of a foreign language *really* requires is not so much rules as understanding.

Experience also shows that the pattern of errors among learners of Spanish is by and large predictable. Most make essentially the same mistakes in the same proportions. To help you to avoid these pitfalls, any aspect of Spanish which is traditionally a cause of frequent errors is presented in this Grammar in a tinted "Note" box. These are areas where special attention is required.

CONTENTS

CONTENTS

CONTENTS

A GLOSSARY OF GRAMMATICAL TERMS

ABSTRACT NOUN An abstract noun is one which refers not to a concrete physical object or a person or animal but to a quality or a concept. Examples of abstract nouns are happiness, life, length.

ACTIVE The active form of a verb is the basic form as in I *remember* her. It contrasts with the *passive* form of the verb as in she will be *remembered*.

ADJECTIVAL NOUN An adjectival noun is an adjective used as a noun. For example, the adjective young is used as a noun in the young at heart.

ADJECTIVE An adjective is a describing word telling us what something or someone is like (eg a *small* house, the *Royal* Family, an *interesting* pastime).

ADVERB Adverbs are normally used with a verb to add extra information by indicating *how* the action is done (adverbs of manner), or *when*, *where* and *to what extent* the action is done (adverbs of time, place and degree). Adverbs may also be used with an adjective or another adverb (eg a *very* attractive girl, *surprisingly* well).

AGREEMENT In Spanish, words such as adjectives, articles and pronouns are said to agree in number and gender with the noun or pronoun they refer to. This means that their form changes according to the *number* of the noun (singular or plural) and its *gender* (masculine or feminine).

APPOSITION A word or a phrase is said to be in apposition to another when it is placed directly after it without any joining word (eg Mr Jones, *our bank manager*, rang today).

ARTICLE   *See* DEFINITE ARTICLE *and* INDEFINITE ARTICLE.

AUGMENTATIVE   An augmentative is an ending added to a noun to indicate largeness or awkwardness, eg un hombr*ón*, una muje*rona*.

AUXILIARY   Auxiliary verbs are used to form compound tenses of other verbs, eg have in I *have* seen or will in she *will* go. The main auxiliary verbs in Spanish are haber, estar and ser.

CARDINAL   Cardinal numbers are numbers such as one, two, ten, fourteen, as opposed to *ordinal* numbers (eg first, second).

CLAUSE   A clause is a group of words which contains at least a *subject* and a *verb*: he said is a clause. A clause often contains more than this basic information, eg he said this to her yesterday. Sentences can be made up of several clauses, eg he said / he'd call me / if he were free. *See* SENTENCE.

COLLECTIVE   A collective noun is one which refers to a group of people or things but which is singular in form. Examples of collective nouns are flock and fleet.

COLLOQUIAL   Colloquial language is the sort of language that can be used in everyday informal conversation but is avoided in formal writing such as legal contracts *etc*.

COMPARATIVE   The comparative forms of adjectives and adverbs are used to compare two or more things, persons or actions. In English, more ... than, -er than, less ... than and as ... as are used for comparison.

COMPLEMENT   The complement is the part of the clause which completes the information on the subject. It may be a noun group (that is *a very difficult question*; she'll make *a good leader*), an adjective group (you seem *tired and stressed*) or a prepositional phrase, that is, a preposition plus a noun group (the cat is *in the garden*).

COMPOUND Compound tenses are verb tenses consisting of more than one element. In Spanish, the compound tenses of a verb are formed by using the *auxiliary* verb with the *present* or *past participle*: estoy hablando, han llegado.

COMPOUND NOUNS Compound nouns are nouns made up of two or more separate words. English examples are **goalkeeper** or **dinner party**. Spanish compound nouns are normally linked by **de**, eg un muro *de* piedra.

CONDITIONAL The conditional *mood* is used to describe what someone would do, or to say what would happen if a condition were fulfilled (eg **I *would come*** if I was well; **the chair *would have broken*** if he **had sat on it**). It is also used to express "future in the past", eg **he said he *would come***.

CONJUGATION The conjugation of a verb is the set of different forms taken in the particular *tenses* and *moods* of that verb.

CONJUNCTION Conjunctions are linking words (eg **and**, **but**, **or**). They may be coordinating or subordinating. Coordinating conjunctions are words like **y**, **o**, **pero**; subordinating conjunctions are words like **que**, **si**, **aunque**.

DEFINITE ARTICLE The definite article is **the** in English and **el**, **la**, **los**, **las** in Spanish.

DEMONSTRATIVE Demonstrative adjectives (eg **this**, **that**, **these**) and pronouns (eg **this one**, **that one**) are used to point out a particular person or thing.

DIMINUTIVE A diminutive is an ending added to a noun (or occasionally to an adjective) to indicate smallness or a favourable attitude on the part of the speaker, eg una mes*ita*, un hij*ito*.

DIRECT OBJECT A direct object is a noun or a pronoun which in English follows a verb without any linking preposition, eg I met *a friend*. Note that in English the preposition before an *indirect object* is often omitted, eg I sent *him* a present – him is equivalent to to him; it is the indirect object – a present is the direct object.

ENDING The ending of a verb is determined by the *person* (1st/2nd/3rd) and *number* (singular/plural) of its subject.

EXCLAMATION Exclamations are words or phrases used to express surprise, annoyance *etc* (eg what!, wow!, how lucky!, what a nice day!). Exclamations in Spanish begin with an upside-down exclamation mark, eg ¡caramba!

FEMININE *See* GENDER.

GENDER The gender of a noun indicates whether the noun is *masculine* or *feminine*. In Spanish, the gender of a noun is not always determined by the sex of what it refers to, eg la víctima (the victim) is a feminine noun, even when it refers to a man.

IDIOM Idioms, or idiomatic expressions, are phrases which cannot normally be translated word for word. For example, it's raining cats and dogs is translated by está lloviendo a cántaros.

IMPERATIVE The imperative *mood* is used for giving orders (eg stop!, don't go!) or for making suggestions (eg let's go).

INDEFINITE Indefinite pronouns are words that do not refer to a definite person or thing (eg each, someone).

INDEFINITE ARTICLE The indefinite article is a in English and un, una in Spanish.

INDICATIVE The indicative *mood* is normally used in making statements or asking questions, as in I *like*, he *came*, we *are trying*. It contrasts with the *subjunctive*, *conditional* and *imperative*.

INDIRECT OBJECT   An indirect object is a pronoun or noun which follows a verb sometimes with a linking preposition (usually to), eg I spoke to *my friend/him*, she gave *him* a kiss.

INFINITIVE   The infinitive is the form of the verb as found in dictionaries. Thus to eat, to finish, to take are infinitives. In Spanish, all infinitives end in -r: tomar, beber, vivir.

INTERROGATIVE   Interrogative words are used to ask a question. They may be used in a direct question (*when* will you arrive?) or an indirect question (I don't know *when* he'll arrive). *See* QUESTION.

MASCULINE   *See* GENDER.

MOOD   Mood is the name given to each of the four main areas within which a verb is conjugated. *See* INDICATIVE, SUBJUNCTIVE, CONDITIONAL, IMPERATIVE.

NEUTER   There are no neuter nouns in Spanish. Only the definite article lo, the pronoun ello and the demonstrative pronouns esto, eso and aquello have a neuter form. The article lo is used with adjectives, eg lo bueno (that which is good, the good thing), and the demonstratives are used to refer to an entire situation, eg no acepto eso (I don't accept that).

NOUN   A noun is a word which refers to living creatures, things, places or abstract ideas, eg postman, cat, shop, passport, life.

NUMBER   The number of a noun indicates whether the noun is *singular* or *plural*. A singular noun refers to one single thing or person (eg boy, train) and a plural noun to several (eg boys, trains).

OBJECT   *See* DIRECT OBJECT, INDIRECT OBJECT.

ORDINAL   Ordinal numbers are numbers such as first, second, third, fourth *etc*, as opposed to *cardinal* numbers (eg one, three).

PASSIVE A verb is used in the passive when the subject of the verb does not perform the action but is subjected to it. In English, the passive is formed by using a part of the verb **to be** and the past participle of the verb, eg he **was rewarded**.

PAST PARTICIPLE The past participle of a verb is the form which is used after **to have** in English to form the perfect tense, eg I have **eaten**, I have **said**, you have **tried**.

PERSON In any tense, there are three persons in the singular (1st: I ..., 2nd: you ..., 3rd: he/she/it ...), and three in the plural (1st: we ..., 2nd: you ..., 3rd: they ...). *See also* ENDING.

PERSONAL PRONOUNS Personal pronouns are used to stand for a noun. In English they are words like **I, you, he/she/it, we, they** or **me, you, him/her/it, us, them**.

PLURAL *See* NUMBER.

POSSESSIVE Possessives are used to indicate possession or ownership. They are words like **my/mine, your/yours, our/ours**.

PREPOSITION Prepositions are words which indicate relationships in space and time, such as **with, in, to, at**. They are normally followed by a noun or a pronoun.

PRESENT PARTICIPLE The present participle is the verb form which ends in **-ing** in English (**-ndo** in Spanish).

PROGRESSIVE The progressive tenses are formed in English by the verb **to be** and the *present participle*, eg I **am speaking**, he **was writing**. In Spanish it is formed by **estar** and the *present participle*, eg estoy hablando, estaba escribiendo.

PRONOUN A pronoun is a word which stands for a noun. The main categories of pronouns are:
- *Personal pronouns* (eg you, him, us)
- *Possessive pronouns* (eg mine, yours, his)
- *Reflexive pronouns* (eg myself, himself)
- *Interrogative pronouns* (eg who?, what?, which?)
- *Relative pronouns* (eg who, which, that)
- *Demonstrative pronouns* (eg this, that, these)
- *Indefinite pronouns* (eg something, none)

QUESTION There are two question forms: *direct* questions stand on their own and require a question mark at the end (eg **when will he come?**); *indirect* questions are introduced by a clause and require no question mark (eg **I wonder *when he will come***). Direct questions begin in Spanish with an upside-down question mark, eg **¿qué haces?**

REFLEXIVE Reflexive verbs 'reflect' the action back onto the subject (eg **I dressed myself**). They are always found with a reflexive pronoun and are more common in Spanish than in English. Verbs are often used reflexively in Spanish where English would use the *passive*.

SENTENCE A sentence is a group of words made up of one or more clauses (*see* CLAUSE). The end of a sentence is indicated by a punctuation mark (usually a full stop, a question mark or an exclamation mark).

SINGULAR *See* NUMBER.

STEM *See* VERB STEM.

SUBJECT The subject of a verb is the *noun* or *pronoun* which performs the action. In the sentences **the train left early** and **she bought a CD**, the train and she are the subjects.

SUBJUNCTIVE The subjunctive is a verb form which is rarely used in English (eg **if I *were* you, God *save* the Queen**). It is very much more common in Spanish.

SUPERLATIVE The superlative is the form of an *adjective* or an *adverb* which, in English, is marked by **the most ...**, **the -est** or **the least ...**.

TENSE Verbs are used in tenses, which indicate when an action takes place, eg in the present, the past, the future.

VERB A verb is a 'doing' word, which usually describes an action (eg **to sing, to work, to watch**). Some verbs describe a state (eg **to be, to have, to hope**).

VERB STEM The stem of a verb is its 'basic unit' to which the various *endings* are added. To find the stem of a Spanish verb remove -ar, -er or -ir from the infinitive. The stem of hablar is *habl*, of beber, *beb*, of vivir, *viv*.

VOICE The two voices of a verb are its *active* and *passive* forms.

PART I
FUNCTIONS

1 REFERRING TO THINGS: THE NOUN

The word 'thing' is used here not just to refer to objects – 'book', 'house', 'car' *etc*, also known as *inanimate* nouns – but also to people and animals – *animate* nouns – and to what are known as *abstract* nouns. Abstract nouns refer not to physical objects but to ideas – 'justice', 'peace', 'democracy' and so on.

A USES OF THE DEFINITE AND INDEFINITE ARTICLES

For the formation of the definite and indefinite articles, see pages 176-8.

There is a considerable degree of agreement between Spanish and English as to when a noun is used with a definite or an indefinite article. However, some important differences also occur.

The traditional terms 'definite article' ('the' in English) and 'indefinite article' ('a', 'an' in English) are to some extent misleading, since it is not necessarily the case that the definite article refers to a specific object (or idea) and the indefinite article does not. For example, in the sentences:

> la casa es vieja
> the house is old

and

> hemos comprado una casa en el campo
> we have bought a house in the country

both nouns refer to a specific house.

Moreover, there are in fact *three* different cases to consider:

cases where the noun is used with a definite article

cases where the noun is used with an indefinite article

cases where the noun is used with no article at all

As you will see later, *truly* indefinite nouns are in fact used without any article in Spanish.

a) Nouns which are used to represent *all* of the thing or things they are referring to – *all* butter, *all* wine, *all* Spaniards and the like – are preceded by the definite article in Spanish:

me gusta la cerveza, pero no me gusta el vino
I like beer (all beer, beer in general), but I don't like wine (wine in general)

los españoles beben mucho vino
Spaniards (all Spaniards) drink a lot of wine

If the noun is used with an adjective or an adjectival phrase, it will still take the definite article if it refers to all of the thing or things indicated by the noun plus the adjective or phrase:

no me gusta el vino tinto
I don't like red wine

Here **el vino tinto** does not represent all wine, but it does stand for all red wine.

los granjeros del sur de España cultivan muchas frutas
farmers in the south of Spain grow a lot of fruit

This refers to all farmers in the south of Spain.

b) Abstract nouns take the definite article in Spanish, since they also refer to the idea as a whole:

la justicia es necesaria si la democracia va a sobrevivir
justice is necessary if democracy is to survive

la inflación está subiendo
inflation is going up

If the abstract noun is used with an adjective, then in some cases it can take the indefinite article:

me miró con una curiosidad creciente
he looked at me with growing curiosity

c) Names of languages take the definite article:

el español es muy interesante, pero no me gusta el francés
Spanish is very interesting, but I don't like French

However, no article is used after en, de and the verbs hablar and estudiar:

el libro está escrito en español   **¿hablas español?**
the book is written in Spanish   do you speak Spanish?

Again, if a particular example of the language is being referred to rather than the language as a whole, the indefinite article is used:

John habla un español excelente
John speaks excellent Spanish (ie the particular Spanish that he speaks is excellent)

d) Names of academic subjects follow the same pattern as in c):

no me gustan las matemáticas, prefiero la física
I don't like maths, I prefer physics

but no article is necessary in the following cases:

he comprado un libro de química
I've bought a chemistry book

estudia matemáticas   **es licenciado en física**
he is studying mathematics   he has a degree in physics

e) Names of illnesses and diseases usually take the definite article, unless the idea of 'a case of' is clearly meant, in which case no article is used:

¿tiene algo contra la laringitis?
do you have anything for laryngitis?

but:

tengo laringitis
I have laryngitis

f) In general physical descriptions names of parts of the body take the definite article:

tiene el pelo castaño y los ojos verdes
she has brown hair and green eyes

However, if the description highlights how one person's eyes *etc* are different from everyone else's, the indefinite article is used:

tiene unos ojos azules que nadie puede resistir
she has blue eyes which no-one can resist

When the part of the body is the subject of the verb the possessive adjective is normally used:

sus ojos son azules como el mar
her eyes are blue like the sea

Note

Where English uses the possessive adjective, Spanish uses the definite article (sometimes together with the indirect object pronouns for greater precision) to indicate possession in relation to parts of the body and items of clothing:

levantó la cabeza he lifted his head	**me duele la cabeza** my head hurts
su madre le lavó la cara his mother washed his face	**se puso el abrigo y salió** he put on his coat and went out

---

g) For reasons of style the definite article is frequently omitted in lists of words, even where you might expect it to appear:

estudio matemáticas, física y química
I study maths, physics and chemistry

B CASES IN WHICH NO ARTICLE IS USED

a) In general, no article is used with the noun if:

the noun does not refer either to the thing as a whole or to a specific example of the thing in question:

me llamó ladrón
he called me a thief

the noun refers to an indefinite amount or number of the thing(s) in question:

no bebo cerveza
I don't drink beer

b) No article is used with general statements of profession or occupation, political or religious conviction, and the like:

mi padre es médico y mi tía es enfermera
my father is a doctor and my aunt is a nurse

ella es católica; él es comunista
she is a Catholic; he is a communist

However, if the noun is made more precise by being used with an adjective, then the indefinite article is used:

su padre es un cirujano conocido
his father is a well-known surgeon

Not all surgeons are famous.

c) Frequently (though not always) when a noun is dependent on a negative or a question no article is used:

¿tienes coche? – no, no tengo coche
have you got a car? – no, I don't have a car

Again, this is not a reference to any particular car. If you did wish to refer to a particular car, you would use the indefinite article:

¿tienes un coche rojo?
do you have a red car?

d) When the noun is used with one of a small number of adjectives the article is omitted. These are otro (other), and tal, semejante and parecido (all meaning 'such'), and cierto (certain, some):

¿me das otro libro, por favor?
would you give me another book, please? (ie any other *undefined* book)

semejante situación nunca se había producido antes
such a situation had never arisen before (a situation of this general kind)

estoy de acuerdo contigo hasta cierto punto
I agree with you up to a point (an *undefined* point)

e) No article is used after qué and vaya in exclamations:

¡qué lástima!	**¡vaya sorpresa!**	**¡vaya paliza!**
what a shame!	what a surprise!	what a bore!

Note that any adjective used in such an exclamation is usually preceded by tan or más:

¡qué día más magnífico!
what a magnificent day!

This más is not considered comparative (*see* page 49), and does not become mejor or peor when used with bueno or malo:

¡qué idea más buena!
what a good idea!

f) No article is used after como in expressions such as the following:

te hablo como amigo
I'm speaking to you as a friend

I am speaking to you not as a particular friend, but as any friend would.

mándenos diez cajas como pedido de prueba
send us ten boxes as a trial order

Compare this with the following:

ya hemos recibido un pedido de prueba de esa empresa
we have already received a trial order from this firm

This is a reference to a specific trial order.

g) The article is not used when expressing indefinite quantities:

¿tienes mantequilla?
do you have (any) butter?

no quiero vino, siempre bebo cerveza
I don't want (any) wine, I always drink beer

Compare this with **la cerveza** in A. a) page 21, which meant 'all beer, beer in general'.

buen número de personas no querían aceptar eso
a good number of people did not want to accept this

parte/buena parte/gran parte del dinero se invirtió en el proyecto
part/a good part/a large part of the money was invested in the project

tengo cantidad/infinidad de preguntas que hacerte
I've got loads/masses of questions to ask you

h) The article is omitted with nouns in apposition:

vive en Madrid, capital de España
he lives in Madrid, the capital of Spain

C NAMES OF PERSONS, COUNTRIES *ETC*

A proper noun is invariably the name of a person, country, continent, organisation or the like. Most proper nouns, including virtually all feminine names of countries, are used without any article in Spanish (*for a list of names of countries which do take the article, see* page 177):

Alemania es un país mucho más rico que España
Germany is a much richer country than Spain

However, the article is used in the following cases:

a) When a person's name is preceded by a title of some kind:

el señor Carballo no estaba
señor Carballo wasn't in

el general Olmeda ya se había marchado
General Olmeda had already left

The exceptions to this are:

- the titles don and doña
- titles used in direct address:

   ¿qué piensa de esto, señor Carballo?
   what do you think of this, señor Carballo?

- foreign titles:

   Lord Byron era un poeta inglés muy conocido
   Lord Byron was a very famous English poet

b) When the noun is used with an adjective:

el pobre Juan no sabía qué hacer
poor Juan didn't know what to do

**esto ha ocurrido muchas veces en la historia de la Europa
   occidental**
this has happened many times in the history of Western
   Europe

However, Gran Bretaña and Estados Unidos have come to be regarded as proper nouns in their own right, so that the definite
articles are no longer used in these cases:

Gran Bretaña votó en contra de la propuesta
Great Britain voted against the proposal

c) Acronyms

An acronym is a name consisting of the initial letters of a
series of words. Known as siglas, these are very widely used
in Spanish. With the exception of certain names of political
parties, siglas always take the definite article, and their gender
is determined by the gender of the first noun in their expanded
form.

A few common acronyms:

la UE	la Unión Europea	the EU
la OTAN	la Organización del Tratado del Atlántico Norte	NATO
el INI	el Instituto Nacional de Industria	Government Department in charge of nationalised industries
el INEM	el Instituto Nacional de Empleo	Department of Employment
el PSOE	el Partido Socialista Obrero Español	Socialist party
IU	Izquierda Unida	Communist-led coalition

España es miembro de la UE
Spain is a member of the EU

España sigue siendo miembro de la OTAN
Spain is still a member of NATO

Even those acronyms which are not names of organizations take the definite article:

el DNI	el Documento Nacional de Identidad	national identity card
la EEB	la Encefalopatía Espongiforme Bovina	BSE
la ESO	la Educación Secundaria Obligatoria	compulsory secondary education
el IVA	el Impuesto sobre el Valor Añadido	VAT

la policía me pidió el DNI
the police asked me for ID

 D THE NEUTER ARTICLE lo

1 Abstract nouns

The neuter article **lo** is used almost exclusively with adjectives and adverbs. When used with an adjective, **lo** transforms the adjective into the corresponding abstract noun. For example lo bueno means 'that which is good'. The translation of such 'nouns' varies according to their context:

   lo esencial es que todos estemos de acuerdo
   the essential thing is for all of us to agree

   lo verdaderamente importante es que todos lo acepten
   what's really important is for everyone to accept it

   los más absurdo es que él no sabía nada
   the most absurd part of it is that he knew nothing

2 Meaning 'how'

Lo + adjective expresses the idea of 'how' in constructions such as the following. Note that in these constructions the adjective agrees with the noun it describes:

   no me había dado cuenta de lo caros que son
   I hadn't realised how expensive they are

If there is no noun, the uninflected form of the adjective is used:

   ¿no ves lo práctico que es?
   can't you see how practical it is?

 ## E USING A VERB AS A NOUN

A verbal noun is a verb used as the subject or object of another verb. In Spanish the *infinitive* is used to express the verbal noun, whereas in English we use the present participle. When used as the subject of a verb, the infinitive is sometimes preceded by the definite article **el**, though it is more common without:

   fumar es peligroso para la salud
   smoking is dangerous for your health

   detesto tener que hacer esto
   I hate having to do this

Note

Under *no* circumstances can a present participle be used as a verbal noun in Spanish as it is in English. Note in particular that the infinitive is the only form of the verb which can come after a preposition in Spanish:

tomó un café antes de salir
he had a coffee before leaving

se sintió mejor después de dormir **un rato**
he felt better after sleeping a while

F SITUATING SOMETHING IN PLACE OR TIME: DEMONSTRATIVES

This function is carried out in Spanish by the demonstrative adjectives and pronouns (*see* page 179). The difference between the three demonstrative adjectives in Spanish is as follows:

1 Used to denote place

- este   refers to something which is close to the speaker
- ese   refers to something which is close to the listener
- aquel   refers to something which is remote from both speaker and listener

   ¿me das ese libro?
   will you give me that book? (= the one near you)

   tomo esta caja
   I'll take this box (= this one I'm holding, pointing to *etc*)

   aquellas flores son muy hermosas
   those flowers are very beautiful (= those over there)

2 Used to denote time

Este is used, as in English, if the *noun* refers to present time:

> **esta semana fuimos a la playa**
> we went to the beach this week

Both ese and aquel can be used to refer to past time with little difference in meaning, though aquel may suggest that the action is more remote:

> **en esa época no se permitían los partidos políticos**
> at that time political parties were not allowed .

> **en aquella época la población de Madrid era de sólo un millón de personas**
> at that time the population of Madrid was only one million

3 'Those who', 'those of'

Note that 'those who' is expressed in Spanish as los que or las que. The actual demonstratives are not used:

> **los que piensan eso se equivocan**
> those who think that are wrong

Likewise, 'that of', 'those of' are expressed as el de, la de, los de, las de. El takes the same contractions as it does when it is used as a definite article – ie a + el becomes al and de + el becomes del (*see* page 177):

> **preferimos las mercancías de Vds. a las de sus competidores**
> we prefer your goods to those of your competitors

> **prefiero el coche de Luis al de Paco**
> I prefer Luis's car to Paco's (to that of Paco)

4 The demonstrative pronouns

For the formation of the demonstrative pronouns, see page 179.

The demonstrative pronouns denote time and place in the same way as the demonstrative adjectives. Note, however, the use of aquél and éste to express the idea of 'the former' and 'the latter':

éste es más difícil que aquél
the latter is more difficult than the former

The neuter demonstrative pronouns esto, eso and aquello are used to represent an unknown object, a general situation, an entire idea.

Note

Demonstrative pronouns can *never* be used to represent a specific noun whose identity is known to the speaker:

¿qué es esto?
what's this? (unknown object)

no puedo aceptar esto
I can't accept this (this situation)

Compare this with:

no puedo aceptar esta situación
I can't accept this situation

G LINKING NOUNS

For a list of coordinating conjunctions, see page 271.

1 y and o

The simplest way of linking nouns is by using the conjunctions y (and) and o (or). Note that y is replaced by e if the pronunciation of the next word begins with the vowel i. It is the pronunciation that is important, not the way the noun is spelled:

padres e hijos
parents and children

Likewise, o is replaced by u if the next word begins with the sound o:

siete u ocho
seven or eight

In the Spanish press, o is frequently written ó between numbers to avoid confusion with the number zero: 60 ó 70.

2 Expressing 'both'

a) 'both' + plural noun

When 'both' is followed by a *single* plural noun, los dos or las dos is used, depending on the gender of the noun. In more formal Spanish, the adjective ambos may be used:

los dos hermanos vinieron/ambos hermanos vinieron
both brothers came

comí las dos tartas/comí ambas tartas
I ate both cakes

> *Note*
>
> Neither los/las dos nor ambos may be used to express the idea of 'both ... and ...' in Spanish.

b) 'both' + two adjectives

'Both' used to link two adjectives referring to the same noun is a la vez:

encuentro este libro a la vez divertido e interesante
I find this book both entertaining and interesting

c) 'both' + two nouns or pronouns

By far the commonest way of expressing 'both ... and ...' linking two dissimilar things in Spanish is tanto ... como .... Since tanto is used as an adverb in this construction, it never changes, no matter what the number or gender of the nouns involved:

tanto tú como yo queremos resolver este problema
both you and I want to solve this problem

2 RELATIONSHIPS BETWEEN THINGS

A PREPOSITIONS

The commonest way of expressing relationships between nouns is by the use of prepositions. *For a detailed list of both simple and compound prepositions and their uses, see* pages 190–200.

The following cases deserve special mention:

1 por and para

As well as having a variety of other meanings, both por and para can be used to express the ideas of 'for' and 'by' in Spanish. Their uses in these meanings can be summarized as follows:

a) Meaning 'for'

   i) In a general sense, it can be said that por refers to *causes*, whereas para refers to *aims* or *objectives*.

   The following examples, both of which mean 'I am doing it for my brother', may clarify the difference:

   lo hago por mi hermano

   Here the emphasis is on what *caused* the speaker to decide to do what he is doing. He is doing it because his brother asked for it to be done, or because his brother needed help in some way.

   Compare with:

   lo hago para mi hermano

   Para here indicates that the action is being done in order to secure some advantage for the brother in the future.

Likewise, the question ¿por qué hiciste esto? asks for an explanation of what caused the action to be done, whereas the question ¿para qué hiciste esto? asks for an explanation of the future objectives.

Here are some other examples showing the distinction between por and para (note that, although the basic ideas remain unchanged, 'for' is not always the best translation in English):

lo hizo por necesidad
he did it out of necessity

cometió el error por cansancio
he made the mistake through tiredness

lo dejaron para otro día
they left it for another day

estamos estudiando para un examen
we're studying for an exam

ii) If there is any idea of an exchange, por is always used:

pagué diez mil euros por este coche
I paid ten thousand euros for this car

voy a cambiar mi viejo coche por otro más moderno
I am going to exchange my old car for a more modern one

iii) To express the idea of 'as regards', 'as far as it concerns', use para:

este libro es demasiado difícil para mí
this book is too difficult for me

tal situación sería inaceptable para España
such a situation would be unacceptable for Spain

b) Meaning 'by'

i) When introducing the person or thing by whom an action was carried out (when using the passive voice), por is always used:

el edificio fue inaugurado por el rey Juan Carlos
the building was inaugurated by King Juan Carlos

ii) When 'by' refers to a future deadline, para is used:

necesitamos las mercancías para finales de octubre
we need the goods by the end of October

2 a and en

Basically a indicates motion *towards* a thing or place, whereas en indicates position *in* or *on* a thing or place. The difference is usually clear in English, but problems can arise when translating the preposition 'at'. If 'at' indicates position *in* or *on*, en must be used:

Juan está en casa
Juan is at home

vi este ordenador en la feria de muestras
I saw this computer at the exhibition

3 antes de, delante de, ante

a) Antes de usually refers to time:

llegamos antes de medianoche
we arrived before midnight

Colloquially, it may also refer to place, though the idea of 'before you arrive at ...' is usually involved:

la iglesia está antes del cruce
the church is before the junction

b) Delante de refers to physical position:

el buzón está delante de Correos
the post box is in front of the Post Office

c) Ante refers to mental position, and is usually used with abstract nouns. It expresses roughly the same idea as the English expressions 'in the presence of', '(when) faced with' and the like:

el gobierno no sabía como reaccionar ante este problema
the government did not know how to react when faced with this problem

There are a few set expressions where ante may refer to physical position, but these are limited and often refer to legal contexts:

compareció ante el juez
he appeared before the judge

POSSESSION

For the formation of the possessive adjectives and pronouns, see
pages 180-1.

The weak forms of the possessive adjectives, which are *by far* the
commonest, are placed before the noun. The strong forms go after
the noun.

1 The weak possessive adjectives

> ## Note
>
> Like any other adjective, the possessive adjective agrees in gender
> and number with the noun it describes. The 'owner' of the things
> described is irrelevant from this point of view:
>
> **¿dónde están nuestras maletas?**
> where are our suitcases?
>
> Nuestras is in the feminine plural form because maletas is feminine
> plural. The owners ('we') could be either male or female.
>
> **los chicos hablaban con su abuelo**
> the boys were speaking with their grandfather
> **las chicas ayudaban a su madre**
> the girls were helping their mother
>
> Su is singular because both abuelo and madre are singular. The
> fact that there were a number of boys or girls does not alter this
> in any way.

2 The strong possessive adjectives

In contemporary Spanish, the strong forms of the possessive
adjectives are for all practical purposes restricted to forms of direct
address, or to expressing the idea 'of mine', 'of yours' *etc*:

> **esto no es posible, amigo mío**
> this is not possible, my friend

unos amigos míos vinieron a verme
some friends of mine came to see me

3 The possessive pronouns

The possessive pronouns take the definite article unless they are used with the verb ser:

¿quieres el mío?
do you want mine?

esta radio no es tuya, es nuestra
this radio isn't yours, it's ours

su casa es mucho más grande que la mía
his house is much bigger than mine

4 Cases where confusion might arise

On occasions, confusion may arise with the use of the adjective su and the pronoun suyo. These forms can mean 'his', 'her(s)', 'your(s)' (singular), 'their(s)', 'your(s)' (plural). In most cases the context will make it clear which meaning is involved. However, if confusion is likely to arise, the following forms can be used instead:

his	**de él**
her(s)	**de ella**
your(s) *(singular)*	**de Vd.**
their(s)	**de ellos, de ellas**
your(s) *(plural)*	**de Vds.**

María no ha perdido su propia maleta , ha perdido la de ellos
María has not lost her own suitcase, she has lost *theirs*

¿es de ella este coche?
is this car hers?

5 Possession in general

There is no equivalent of the English 'apostrophe s' in Spanish.
Possession is expressed in various ways, the most common being
the use of the preposition de. The order in which the nouns are
expressed is the exact opposite of English:

el amigo de mi padre
my father's friend

Note that de + el becomes del:

el primo del amigo del profesor
the teacher's friend's cousin

6 Expressing 'whose'

'Whose' in a question is ¿de quién?

¿de quién es este lápiz?
whose is this pencil?

In an adjectival clause, 'whose' is expressed by the adjective cuyo,
which agrees with the thing owned:

el hombre cuya ventana rompieron está furioso
the man whose window they broke is furious

la mujer cuyos hijos se fueron
the woman whose children went away

7 The verb pertenecer

Possession of objects can sometimes be expressed by the use of the
verb pertenecer (to belong). However, this is rather formal and is
much less common than the use of de:

¿a quién pertenece esto? – pertenece al profesor
whose is this? – it's the teacher's

The more common meaning of **pertenecer** is 'belong' in the sense of 'be a member of':

pertenece al partido socialista
he belongs to the socialist party

8 With parts of the body and items of clothing

When used as the object of a verb, parts of the body and items of clothing take the definite article, not the possessive adjective as in English. The 'owner' is often indicated by means of the indirect object pronoun:

su madre le lavó la cara
his mother washed his face

se quemó la mano
he burned his hand
(= his own hand)

 C COMPOUND NOUNS

A compound noun consists of a group of nouns which go together to define something more precisely, eg 'kitchen table', 'bedroom carpet'.

a) Using **de**

In Spanish, the elements of a compound noun are usually joined by a preposition, which will in most cases be **de**:

una pared de piedra
a stone wall

un portavoz del ministerio de energía
an energy department spokesman

Note that the order in which the nouns are expressed is again the opposite of English, and that the gender of the compound noun in Spanish is based on the gender of the first noun:

un sombrero de paja viejo
an old straw hat (**viejo** agrees with **sombrero** and not with **paja**)

b) Other compounds

In recent years a number of compound nouns have appeared in Spanish which do not have a preposition of any kind. The two nouns simply appear side by side, or are joined by a hyphen. Such nouns take the gender of the first noun, and are also made plural by making the first noun plural:

un coche-bomba	**coches-bomba**
a car bomb	car bombs
la fecha límite	**fechas límite**
the closing date	closing dates
un retrato robot	**retratos robot**
an Identikit portrait	Identikit portraits

You should beware of inventing your own compound nouns of this type. Use only those you know for certain to exist. Otherwise always use the construction with de as described above.

3 DESCRIBING THINGS

A AUGMENTATIVES AND DIMINUTIVES

For the formation of augmentatives and diminutives, see pages 182-3.

A particular characteristic of Spanish is to suggest a different view of something by adding either an augmentative or a diminutive to the end of the noun. Both augmentatives and diminutives can have a merely physical meaning, or they can introduce more subjective elements into the way in which the noun is presented.

Both augmentatives and diminutives require a certain amount of care in Spanish, and the learner should beware of inventing his own at random. Use only those of whose connotations you are sure.

1 Diminutives

Diminutives are widely used in spoken Spanish, though they are much less common in formal written Spanish, and would frequently be out of place there. They may simply express size, but they more often suggest a favourable/unfavourable attitude of the speaker towards what he is describing. There is often no simple translation for a diminutive used in this way.

a) Size

había una mesita en el rincón
there was a small table in the corner

un momentito, por favor
just a moment, please

b) Favourable attitude

This is expressed primarily by the diminutive -ito, which is the commonest of all the diminutives:

me miraba con la carita cubierta de lágrimas
he looked at me with his face covered in tears

'hola', me dijo con su vocecita encantadora
'hello', she said in her charming little voice

c) Unfavourable attitude

This is expressed by the diminutive -uelo which is comparatively rare:

pasamos por dos o tres aldehuelas sin interés
we passed through two or three uninteresting little villages

2 Augmentatives

Augmentatives indicate mostly size, though sometimes the idea of clumsiness or even ugliness may also be implied:

llegó un hombrón y se puso a trabajar
a big fellow arrived and started to work

un hombrote/hombrazo/hombracho
a big brute of a fellow

una mujerona
a big strong woman

Some augmentatives and diminutives have now become words in their own right and no longer have any of the connotations mentioned above:

el sillón
armchair

la tesina
dissertation

el gatillo
trigger

B THE ADJECTIVE

1 Agreement

For the formation of the feminine and plural of adjectives, see **pages 185-6.**

All adjectives in Spanish must agree both in gender and number with the noun they are describing:

las paredes eran blancas, y el suelo era blanco también
the walls were white, and the floor was white as well

If a single adjective refers to a mixture of masculine and feminine nouns, it takes the masculine plural form:

las paredes y el suelo eran blancos
the walls and the floor were white

If a plural noun is followed by two or more adjectives and each adjective refers to only one of the things mentioned in the noun, each adjective may take the singular form:

los partidos socialista y comunista votaron en contra de la ley
the socialist and communist parties voted against the bill

(there is only one socialist party and one communist party)

2 Lists of adjectives

A number of adjectives may be used to describe the same noun, as in English. Those adjectives considered most important should be placed closest to the noun. This will usually result in an order of adjectives in Spanish which is the exact opposite of English:

un diputado socialista español conocido
a well-known Spanish socialist MP

la política agraria común europea
the European common agricultural policy

3 Choice of position

Although most adjectives usually follow the noun, they can be placed in front of the noun for emphasis. This option is widely used in contemporary written Spanish, though it is less common in spoken Spanish:

> **este equipo da una fiel reproducción del sonido original**
> this equipment gives a faithful reproduction of the original sound

This is very much a question of style, and should be used with caution unless you have seen or heard the particular example you wish to use.

C THE INDEFINITE ADJECTIVES

For the forms of alguno *and* cualquiera *see* pages 184–5.

1 'Some'

In the singular, the adjective alguno means 'some' in the sense of 'some ... or other':

> **compró el libro en alguna librería**
> he bought the book in some bookshop (or other)

In the plural it simply means 'some'. In this case it can be replaced without change of meaning by the appropriate form of unos/unas:

> **vinieron algunos/unos hombres y se pusieron a trabajar**
> some men turned up and started to work

2 'Any'

Both the adjective alguno and the adjective cualquiera can be translated into English as 'any', and the difference between the two is often difficult for the English-speaking learner to grasp.

Alguno in this sense appears mostly in questions, and is used to find out whether a specific thing or group of things actually exists.

Cualquiera, on the other hand, refers in a completely indefinite way to things which are known to exist. It expresses much the same idea as the English phrases 'any at all', 'any whatsoever'.

Compare the following:

> **¿hay alguna librería por aquí?**
> are there any bookshops around here?

and

> **puedes encontrar este libro en cualquier librería**
> you can find this book in any bookshop

The first phrase asks whether any bookshops actually exist in the area. (Note that *in a question* alguno is almost always used in the *singular* in Spanish, even when a plural would normally be used in English).

The second sentence means that you can buy the book in any bookshop whatsoever: it is assumed that there are indeed bookshops available.

In other cases, the logic of the statement will require one adjective to be used rather than the other:

> **cualquier mecánico podría hacer eso**
> any mechanic could do that

ie any mechanic at all; algún would not make any sense in this context.

Note that very often English 'any' is not translated into Spanish:

> **¿tiene mantequilla?**   **no tenemos plátanos**
> do you have any butter?   we don't have any bananas

The order of 'indefiniteness' in Spanish is as follows:

alguna librería	some bookshop (or other)
algunas/unas librerías	some bookshops
cualquier librería	any bookshop whatsoever
librerías	bookshops

D VARYING THE FORCE OF AN ADJECTIVE

1 Diminutives and augmentatives

It is possible to add diminutives, and in a small number of cases augmentatives, to certain adjectives. The connotations involved are as for nouns. This feature requires extra special care. Use only those you know to exist and about which you feel confident:

el agua está calentita hoy
the water is nice and warm today

¡qué tontita eres!
how silly you are!

el niño está muy grandón
the child is very big (for his age)

2 Adverbs

A whole range of adverbs can be used to vary the force of an adjective.

For the formation of adverbs, see **page 208.**

For a list of adverbs of degree, see **pages 212–13.**

Any adjective modified by an adverb in this way *must* go after the noun, even if the simple form normally precedes the noun:

me dió un libro sumamente interesante
he gave me an extremely interesting book

> *Note*
>
> It is essential to remember that adverbs are *invariable*, that is they *never* change their form, no matter what the gender or number of the adjective they modify.

3 Increasing the force of the adjective

encuentro todo esto muy aburrido
I find all of this very boring

Muy cannot be used on its own. If there is no adjective to follow it, it is replaced by mucho. In this case mucho is used as an adverb and never changes its form:

¿encontraste interesante la revista? – sí, mucho
did you find the magazine interesting? – yes, very

este libro es sumamente (*or* extremamente *or* extremadamente) interesante
this book is extremely interesting

4 Decreasing the force of the adjective

The adverb poco is used to lessen or even *negate* the force of an adjective:

me parece poco probable que venga
it seems unlikely to me that he will come

Note

Do not confuse poco with un poco, which means 'a little', 'a bit'. Compare:

la sopa está poco caliente   **la sopa está un poco caliente**
the soup is not very hot   the soup is a little hot

E COMPARING THINGS: THE COMPARATIVE AND THE SUPERLATIVE

THE COMPARATIVE

For the formation of comparatives, see pages 187-8.

1 Simple comparison

a) The comparison of equality (one thing is as good, as interesting *etc* as another)

If the comparison is based on an adjective, it is expressed by
tan + adjective + como:

Juan es tan alto como su hermana
Juan is as tall as his sister

Luisa no es tan trabajadora como su hermana
Luisa isn't as hard-working as her sister

If the comparison is based on a noun (ie it is one of quantity –
'as much as', 'as many as'), it is expressed by tanto + noun +
como. Tanto is used as an adjective here and therefore agrees
with the noun:

yo tengo tantos discos como tú
I have as many records as you

b) The comparison of superiority (one thing is better, longer *etc*
than another)

When the comparison is based on an adjective, the construction
más + adjective + que is used (*see* **page 187** *for irregular comparatives*):

María es más inteligente que su hermano
María is cleverer than her brother

If the comparison is one of quantity, the construction más +
noun + que is used:

ellos tienen más dinero que nosotros
they have more money than us

If the comparison is made with a specific number or amount, de
is used instead of que:

vinieron más de cien personas
more than one hundred people came

esperamos más de media hora
we waited for over half an hour

c) The comparison of inferiority (one thing is less good, less
interesting than another)

The comparison of inferiority is expressed by menos. It follows the same patterns as the comparison of superiority:

esta revista es menos interesante que aquélla
this magazine is less interesting than that one

tú haces menos errores que yo
you make fewer mistakes than me

pagué menos de cien euros
I paid less than a hundred euros

d) Note that, whereas English uses the terms 'ever' and 'anyone' in a comparison, Spanish uses the corresponding *negative* terms:

la situación es más grave que nunca
the situation is more serious than ever

él sabe más que nadie
he knows more than anyone

Other indefinite comparisons are usually expressed by using the adjective cualquiera (*see* page 185):

Isabel es más inteligente que cualquier otro estudiante
Isabel is more intelligent than any other student

2 Comparison with a clause

When the comparison is being made not with a noun but with a clause, que is replaced by more complex forms.

a) Comparison based on an adjective

When the comparison is based on an adjective, the clause is introduced by de lo que:

la situación es más compleja de lo que piensas
the situation is more complex than you think

el problema era más difícil de lo que habían dicho
the problem was more difficult than they had said

b) Comparison based on a noun (ie comparison of quantity)

In this case, the appropriate form of del que, de la que, de los que, de las que is used. The form chosen must agree in gender and number with the noun:

vinieron más personas de las que esperábamos
more people came than we expected

surgieron más problemas de los que habíamos previsto
more problems arose than we had foreseen

The los in de los que agrees with problemas, which is masculine.

gasté más dinero del que ahorré
I spent more money than I saved

The el in del que agrees with dinero.

3 Other phrases of comparison

a) 'More and more' is expressed in Spanish by the phrase cada vez más:

encuentro su comportamiento cada vez más extraño
I find his behaviour more and more odd

Vez may be replaced by another word indicating time without the idea of 'more and more' being lost:

la situación se pone cada día más grave
the situation is becoming more and more serious every day

'Less and less' is cada vez menos:

encuentro sus explicaciones cada vez menos verosímiles
I find his explanations less and less plausible

b) 'The more/less ... the more/less ...' is expressed by cuanto + comparative ... tanto + comparative ... If used with an adjective or adverb cuanto is invariable, but agrees in comparisons of quantity (ie with nouns).

In all cases the **tanto** can be omitted, and it is in fact more common to omit it:

cuanto más fáciles son los ejercicios, más le gustan
the easier the exercises are, the more he likes them

cuanto más dinero tiene, más quiere
the more money he has, the more he wants

cuantos menos problemas tengamos, más contento estaré
the fewer problems we have, the happier I'll be

c) 'All the more' + adjective + 'because' is expressed in Spanish as **tanto** + comparative + **cuanto que**. This construction is limited to very formal Spanish:

esto es tanto más importante cuanto que nos queda poco tiempo
this is all the more important because we don't have much time

THE SUPERLATIVE

For the formation of superlatives, see page 189.

1 The relative superlative

a) The relative superlative is used to express one thing's superiority over all others of its kind:

el español es la asignatura más interesante de las que estudio
Spanish is the most interesting subject I study

Luisa se puso su mejor traje
Luisa put on her best suit

b) The scope of the superlative

The preposition **de** is used to introduce the scope of the superlative, whereas in English we use 'in':

es el hombre más rico de la ciudad
he's the richest man in town

Estados Unidos es el país más poderoso del mundo
The United States is the most powerful country in the world

c) Order of superlatives

A descending order of superlatives ('the second oldest man', 'the third richest woman') is expressed as follows:

el segundo hombre más viejo
the second oldest man

la tercera mujer más rica
the third richest woman

2 The absolute superlative

It is important to distinguish clearly in Spanish between the relative superlative used to compare one thing with others, and the absolute superlative which refers only to one thing without reference to others (*for the formation of the absolute superlative see* **page** 189):

eso es rarísimo
that's most unusual

No comparison is involved here – the statement is simply that something is *very* unusual.

The absolute superlative can also be expressed by one of the adverbs of intensity:

encuentro esto sumamente interesante
I find this most interesting

F ADJECTIVAL PHRASES

Spanish, like English, can use a wide range of adjectival phrases to describe a noun. Such phrases are often the only way to translate certain compound adjectives into Spanish. They consist mostly of nouns introduced by the preposition de though other prepositions do occur:

un hombre de dos metros de altura
a man two metres tall

una mujer de pelo rubio y ojos azules
a fair-haired, blue-eyed woman

refugiados sin casa ni dinero
homeless, penniless refugees

G ADJECTIVAL CLAUSES

Adjectival clauses are used to describe things. The thing being described is referred to as the 'antecedent'. Like all clauses, an adjectival clause *must* contain a verb.

> ### Note
>
> Unlike English, *all* adjectival clauses in Spanish *must* be introduced by a relative pronoun. Omitting the relative pronoun will make it difficult for Spanish speakers to understand you.

For the formation of the relative pronouns, see page 201.

1 The relative pronoun que

In most cases, the simple relative pronoun que can be used:

los hombres que están charlando son españoles
the men who are chatting are Spanish

¿viste la película que pusieron ayer?
did you see the film (that/which) they put on yesterday?

2 Adjectival clauses with prepositions

Note that a preposition can never appear at the end of an adjectival clause in Spanish: such a construction is meaningless. Any preposition must be placed before the relative pronoun:

los muchachos con quienes jugaba se han marchado
the boys he was playing with (with whom he was playing) have gone away

la carta en que leí esto por primera vez está en la mesa
the letter I read this in for the first time (the letter in which I read this ...) is on the table

If the antecedent is a *person*, que may not be used. It is usually replaced by quien (or plural quienes), though the appropriate forms of el que or el cual are also sometimes used:

el hombre con quien hablaba es mi tío
the man I was speaking with is my uncle

los turistas a quienes vendí mi coche
the tourists I sold my car to

If the antecedent is a *thing*, the following rules apply:

a) If the relative pronoun is preceded by a compound preposition (ie one consisting of more than one word, eg detrás de), one of the compound forms of the relative pronoun must be used. You must choose the form of el que or el cual which agrees in number and gender with the antecedent:

la casa detrás de la cual se encuentra el lago
the house behind which the lake is to be found

el árbol debajo del cual nos besamos
the tree under which we kissed

Since the el que and el cual forms are in fact forms of the definite article followed by que or cual, the usual contractions occur (*see* page 177):

el edificio delante del cual esperábamos
the building we were waiting in front of

preferimos tu nuevo coche al que tenías antes
we prefer your new car to the one you had before

b) After the simple prepositions de, en, con *etc*, que may be used, though in more formal Spanish the compound forms are often preferred in such cases:

la casa en que vivimos es muy vieja
the house we live in is very old

3 lo que, lo cual

If the antecedent is not an identifiable thing or things, but refers instead to an entire situation or an idea, then the neuter forms lo que or lo cual *must* be used. They are interchangeable:

Juan insistió en acompañarnos, lo que no me gustó nada
Juan insisted on coming with us, which did not please me at all

What displeased you was not Juan, but the fact that he insisted on coming along.

María se negó a hacerlo, lo que no entiendo
María refused to do it, which I don't understand

Again, it is not María that you do not understand, but the fact that she refused to do it.

4 Adjectival clauses with an indefinite or negative antecedent

An adjectival clause has an indefinite antecedent if the noun being described refers to something (object/person/idea) which *may or may not exist*.

The antecedent is negative if the noun being described refers to something which *does not exist*.

Note that in both these cases, the verb in the adjectival clause must be in the *subjunctive* (present or imperfect depending on the context).

For the formation of the subjunctive, see pages 228-31.

a) Indefinite antecedents
   busco a alguien que hable español
   I am looking for someone who can speak Spanish

This person may not exist – you may not find him or her. Compare this with busco a un hombre que habla español, where the use of the indicative habla indicates that you know a specific gentleman who in fact speaks Spanish, but you just cannot find him at the moment.

los que no quieran participar pueden irse ahora
those who don't wish to take part can leave now

There is no way of telling how many people will not want to take part. In fact everyone might want to take part.
This construction is frequently used with adjectival clauses which refer to the future:

los que no lleguen a tiempo no podrán entrar
those who don't arrive on time will not be allowed in

Obviously, everyone might arrive on time.
In formal Spanish, quien is used on its own as an indefinite relative pronoun meaning 'someone (who)', 'anyone (who)'. It can be either the subject or the object of the adjectival clause:

busco quien me ayude
I am looking for someone to help me (who can help me)

quien diga eso no entiende nada
anyone who says that understands nothing

b) Negative antecedents

no hay nadie que sepa hacerlo
there is no-one who knows how to do it

no tengo libro que te valga
I haven't got any books which would be any use to you

no conozco ningún país donde permitan eso
I don't know any country where they allow that

4 REFERRING TO ACTIONS: THE VERB

The word 'actions' is used here not just to refer to actions as they are normally understood. It also includes mental activities such as 'thinking', 'considering' and the like, as well as states such as 'being', 'seeming', 'appearing' and so on.

A WHO IS PERFORMING THE ACTION?: THE SUBJECT

1 The subject pronoun

For the subject pronouns, see page 202.

a) Cases where the subject pronoun is not stated

In English, the subject of the verb is either explicitly stated – 'my friend went back to Spain yesterday' – or it is replaced by a pronoun – 'he went back to Spain yesterday'.

However, the ending of the verb in Spanish usually makes it clear who the subject is – for example hablo can only mean 'I speak', hablamos can only mean 'we speak'. Consequently, it is also possible in Spanish to use the verb on its own without a subject pronoun:

¿qué piensas de todo esto?
what do you think of all this?

iremos a la playa mañana
we'll go to the beach tomorrow

This is in fact more common than using the subject pronoun with the verb. However, **Vd.** and **Vds.** are used more frequently than

other pronouns. This is to avoid confusion with, for example,
él/ella and ellos/ellas since the verb endings are the same.

¿por qué estudia Vd. español?
why are you studying Spanish?

Note that the subject pronoun is also not used in constructions
such as the following:

los escoceses preferimos el whisky
we Scots prefer whisky

los españoles bebéis mucho vino
you Spaniards drink a lot of wine

b) Use of the subject pronouns

However, the subject pronouns *are* expressed (1) for emphasis or
(2) where obvious confusions would arise:

¿qué piensas tú de todo esto?
what do *you* think of all this?

él salió al cine, pero ella se quedó en casa
he went out to the cinema, but she stayed at home

If the pronouns were not expressed here, it would not be clear
who did what.

Remember that nosotros, vosotros and ellos have feminine forms
which must be used if only girls or women are involved:

María y Carmen, ¿qué pensáis vosotras de esto?
María and Carmen, what do you think of this?

Note also the difference between Spanish and English in
constructions such as the following:

¿quién es? – soy yo/somos nosotros
who is it? – it's me/it's us

soy yo quien quiere hacerlo
it's me who wants to do it

As can be seen, the verb ser agrees here with its expressed
subject.

c) ello

Ello is a *neuter* pronoun in Spanish and can *never* be used to refer to a specific object. It is used to refer to an entire idea or situation. Its use as a genuine subject is rare and is by and large restricted to a few constructions in formal Spanish:

todo ello me parece extraño
all of that seems very strange to me

Ello here refers to a situation which has just been described.

por ello decidió no continuar
he therefore decided not to continue

d) Emphasising the subject pronoun

The subject pronouns are emphasised by using the appropriate form of the adjective mismo:

lo hice yo mismo
I did it myself

A woman saying this would obviously say lo hice yo misma.

me lo dijeron ellos mismos
they told me so themselves

e) tú and usted

Traditionally, tú has been reserved for close friends and relatives, and children, usted being used in any more formal situation. However, there is little doubt that the use of tú has increased dramatically in Spain in recent years, and any young person going to Spain can confidently expect to be automatically addressed as tú by people of his or her own age, and should also respond using tú.

Even the not-so-young will find themselves addressed as tú by people they have never spoken to before. However, a certain amount of caution is still required. When addressing an older person, or someone in authority, for the first time, usted is certainly to be recommended. In general, you should take your

REFERRING TO ACTIONS: THE VERB

lead from the Spaniards you are talking to. If everyone is using tú, it would be silly (and unfriendly) to persist with usted.

2 The indefinite subject

In colloquial English, the indefinite subject is expressed as 'you' and less frequently as 'they'. In more formal spoken and written English, it is expressed as 'one'. In Spanish it can be expressed in the following ways:

a) Use of tú

In colloquial Spanish the tú forms of the verb can also be used to express an indefinite subject:

bajas por esta calle y tomas la primera a la izquierda
you go down this street and you take the first on the left

Like its English equivalent, this is not a reference to the person addressed, but is a truly indefinite subject.

In formal spoken and in written Spanish, however, this construction would be out of place. Two alternative constructions are available, as follows.

b) Reflexive use of the verb

se dice que los precios en España son muy bajos
they say that prices are low in Spain

se cree que habrá menos turistas este año
they think there will be fewer tourists this year

c) The use of uno or la gente

uno no puede por menos de reírse
one cannot help laughing

la gente no cree todo lo que dice el gobierno
people don't believe everything the government says

Either uno or la gente is obligatory if the verb itself is used reflexively:

a la larga uno se acostumbra a todo
you can get used to anything in the long run

3 Agreement of subject and verb

The verb in Spanish *must* agree in number and person with the subject.

Remember in particular that nouns such as la gente, el gobierno and phrases such as todo el mundo are grammatically *singular*. They may be logical plurals (ie they refer to a number of people), but they are singular nouns and *must* take a singular verb:

> **la gente no quiere que el gobierno haga eso**
> people don't want the government to do that

> **todo el mundo lo sabe**
> everyone knows it

La mayoría and la mayor parte (both meaning 'the majority', 'most') take a singular verb. However, if they are followed by a second plural noun, the verb is usually plural:

> **la mayoría votó en contra de la propuesta**
> the majority voted against the proposal

> **la mayoría de los diputados votaron en contra de la propuesta**
> most of the MPs voted against the proposal

On the other hand, there are a small number of plural nouns which are perceived as referring to a singular object, and which are regularly followed by a singular verb:

> **Estados Unidos ha expresado su desacuerdo con esta decisión**
> the United States has expressed its disagreement with this decision

Estados Unidos is treated here simply as the name of a country. This also occurs with the name of the trade union Comisiones Obreras:

> **Comisiones Obreras se opuso a la política del gobierno**
> Comisiones Obreras opposed the government's policy

However, if the article were used, the verb would indeed be plural:

> **los Estados Unidos no están de acuerdo**
> the United States are not in agreement

Note also that if the verb ser is followed by a plural noun, it is itself plural, even if its apparent subject is singular:

el problema son los elevados precios del petróleo
the problem is the high prices of petrol

B TO WHOM IS THE ACTION BEING DONE?: THE OBJECT

1 Direct and indirect objects

If the action of a verb applies *directly* to a person or thing, that person or thing is the *direct object* of the verb.

If the action does not apply directly, but the idea of 'to someone or something' or 'for someone or something' is involved (even if this idea is not explicitly expressed) then the person or thing is the *indirect object* of the verb.

A verb can have both a direct and an indirect object at the same time:

le escribí una carta a mi hermano
I wrote a letter to my brother

In this sentence carta is the direct object since it is the letter which is written, and hermano is the indirect object since it is the brother that the letter is written *to*.

a) 'to' or 'for'

This can sometimes be confusing for an English-speaking learner of Spanish because the difference between direct and indirect objects is not always clear in English, whereas it must *always* be clearly signalled in Spanish. Take the following examples:

I gave the dog to my brother
I gave the dog a bone

In the first sentence, 'the dog' is the direct object of the verb 'give', since the dog is what you actually gave, and 'brother' is the indirect object, since you gave the dog *to* your brother.

In the second sentence, 'the dog' is no longer the direct object, since here you are not giving the dog at all. What you are giving is 'a bone', and 'bone' is now the direct object. You gave the bone *to* the dog, so 'the dog' is now the *indirect* object.

Although 'the dog' has changed from being the direct to the indirect object, there is nothing in the words used in English to indicate this change.

This is not the case in Spanish. An indirect object is *always* clearly marked in Spanish by being preceded by the preposition a. Consequently the Spanish translation of the sentences given above is:

le di el perro a mi hermano
le di un hueso al perro

(*For the use of the pronoun* le *here, see* page 66.)

As can be seen, if both nouns are expressly stated in Spanish (as opposed to being replaced by pronouns), the direct object precedes the indirect object.

b) 'from'

Unlike English, Spanish uses an indirect object to indicate the person *from* whom something is taken, stolen, bought or hidden:

le compré el coche a mi padre
I bought the car from my father

le robó el dinero a su madre
he stole the money from his mother

trataron de ocultar la verdad al profesor
they tried to hide the truth from the teacher

2 The personal a

> ### Note
>
> If the direct object of a verb is a particular person or a particular group of people, it is essential to precede it in Spanish by the preposition a:
>
> **veo a mi hermano**   **encontré a mi padre**
> I can see my brother   I met my father
>
> Note that this a does not transform the direct object into an indirect object. This a is not translated in English.

If the direct object is a person but is not a *particular* person, the a is not used:

> **buscamos un médico**
> we are looking for a doctor

(ie not a particular doctor, but any doctor at all)

The personal a is also used with certain pronouns referring to people, even though these may not always refer to specific people:

> **conozco a alguien que puede ayudarte**
> I know someone who can help you
>
> **no veo a nadie**
> I can't see anyone

The personal a is also used with animals if it is a specific animal which is being referred to:

> **llevé a mi perro a dar un paseo**
> I took my dog for a walk

3 The object pronouns

The function of a pronoun is to stand for a noun. For example, in the sentence 'John wanted the book, so I gave it to him', 'it' stands for 'the book', and 'him' stands for 'John'.

REFERRING TO ACTIONS: THE VERB

For the forms of the object pronouns, see **pages 202-3.**

a) Direct and indirect object pronouns

> ### Note
>
> The direct object pronoun can only stand for the direct object of a verb as explained above. If there is any idea of 'to' or 'for', the indirect object pronoun must be used in Spanish, even though the words 'to' or 'for' may not actually be used in the equivalent English expression.
>
> This does not apply with verbs of motion – for example ir a – or where the idea of 'to' or 'for' is contained in the verb – for example buscar, meaning 'to look for' (*for a list of such verbs, see* **pages 257-8**).
>
> **le dí el dinero**
> I gave him/her the money (I gave the money to him/her)
> **les ofreció diez mil euros**
> he offered them ten thousand euros (he offered ten thousand euros to them)
> **le mandé una carta ayer**
> I sent her a letter yesterday (I sent a letter to her)

In both spoken and written Spanish, the third person indirect object pronoun is almost always used even when the indirect object is explicitly stated:

le dí el libro a mi amigo
I gave the book to my friend

él *se* lo dio a su hermano
he gave it to his brother

b) le and lo as direct object pronouns

Strictly speaking, le is used as the direct object referring to a man or boy (a masculine *person*), whereas lo is used as the direct object referring to a masculine *thing*:

¿ves a mi hermano? – sí, sí, le veo
can you see my brother? – yes, yes, I can see him

¿ves el libro? – sí, sí, lo veo
can you see the book? – yes, yes, I can see it

However, in spoken Spanish, and occasionally also in written Spanish, these forms are often mixed up, giving rise to what is known as loísmo (the use of lo for le):

¿ves a mi hermano? – sí, sí, lo veo
can you see my brother? – yes, yes, I can see him

The use of le for lo, or les for los in the plural, also occurs (leísmo):

¿tienes los libros? – sí, les tengo
have you got the books? – yes, I've got them

You will almost certainly come across these at some point, though it is probably best not to imitate them.

4 The neuter pronoun lo

The neuter pronoun lo can never refer to an identifiable person or thing. It refers only to a whole idea or situation:

¿sabes que ha llegado Juan? – sí, ya lo sé
do you know that Juan has arrived? – yes, I do (I know it)

What you know is that 'Juan has arrived'. Lo in this sense often translates 'so' in English:

tú mismo me lo dijiste
you told me so yourself

Lo can also be used after either of the verbs 'to be' (ser and estar). In this case it usually refers back to the last adjective, though in the case of ser it can also refer back to a noun.

Remember that lo *never* changes its form, no matter what the gender or number of the adjective or noun to which it refers:

ellos están cansados, y nosotros lo estamos también
they are tired, and so are we

The pronoun lo in the example above refers back to cansados.

> **su padre es médico, y el mío lo es también**
> his father is a doctor, and so is mine

The pronoun lo here refers back to the noun médico.

5 The strong object pronouns

For the forms of the strong object pronouns, see page 203.

The strong pronouns are used after prepositions:

> **¿este dinero es para mí? – no, es para ellos**
> is this money for me? – no, it's for them

The strong pronouns are also used with the preposition a to lend emphasis to direct or indirect pronouns which are stated in the same sentence:

> **me dio el libro a mí, no a ti**
> he gave the book to *me*, not to you

> **te veo a ti, pero no la veo a ella**
> I can see you, but I can't see her

This emphasis can be further heightened by placing the strong pronoun before the verb:

> **a mí no me gusta nada**
> *I* don't like it at all

C EMPHASISING THE ACTION

In English all verb tenses have two forms – the standard form ('I read') and the progressive form ('I am reading'). As well as this, the present and past tenses have an emphatic form ('I do read', 'I did read'), which is used to give special emphasis to the verb. In Spanish, only the standard and progressive forms of the verb are available.

If you wish to emphasise the verb, other constructions must be used, for example:

sí que te creo or **te aseguro que te creo**
I *do* believe you

ella sí que no vendrá or **seguro que ella no vendrá**
she definitely won't come

Occasionally an action is emphasised by using first the infinitive and then the appropriate part of the verb:

¿tú bebes? – beber no bebo, pero fumo mucho
do you drink? – I don't drink, but I smoke a lot

D NEGATING THE ACTION

1 Simple negation

In simple negation, *no* is placed in front of the verb:

no leo muchas revistas, no me gustan
I don't read many magazines, I don't like them

no le vi porque no vino
I didn't see him because he didn't come

2 Compound negation

With compound negatives, two possibilities are usually available:

a) *no* is placed in front of the verb and the other negative is placed after the verb; in most cases this construction is preferred:

no conozco a nadie aquí　　　**no sabe nada**
I don't know anyone here　　　　he doesn't know anything

Note that this does *not* constitute a 'double negative' as in English. This applies even when the second negative is in a different clause:

no quiero que hables con nadie
I don't want you to speak to anyone

no es necesario que hagas nada
it isn't necessary for you to do anything

b) no is omitted and the negative is placed before the verb on its own; by and large this construction is usually confined to uses of nadie as subject of the verb, and to tampoco, nunca and jamás:

nadie sabe adonde ha ido
no-one knows where he has gone

Luisa nunca llega a tiempo
Luisa never arrives on time

a mí tampoco me gusta
I don't like it either

Note that 'también no' is not used in Spanish.

3 Other negatives

The phrases estar sin + infinitive and estar por + infinitive negate the action in a way which can suggest that it has *not yet* been done:

la puerta está todavía sin reparar
the door hasn't been repaired yet

este problema está todavía por resolver
this problem has still to be solved

Estar can be replaced by quedar:

queda mucho trabajo por hacer
there's still a lot of work to do

4 Negatives after prepositions

Note that the prepositions sin and antes de are followed by negatives whereas in English they are followed by the corresponding positive term:

salió sin hablar con nadie
he went out without speaking to anyone

decidió comer algo antes de hacer nada más
he decided to eat something before doing anything else

5 More than one negative

A number of negatives may be used together in Spanish as in English. In English, however, only the first term is negative.

In Spanish, *all* terms are negative:

nadie sabe nunca nada
no-one ever knows anything

no hablo nunca con nadie
I never speak to anyone

6 Emphasising the negative (nouns)

With nouns, the negative can be emphasised by using the negative adjective ninguno (*see* page 184). Ninguno is seldom used in the plural:

no me queda ningún dinero
I have no money left

For added emphasis, the appropriate form of alguno may be placed *after* the noun:

no tiene miedo alguno
he's not the least bit afraid

In colloquial Spanish, nada de can also be used before the noun:

no me queda nada de dinero
I have no money left at all

The order of 'negativeness' in Spanish is:

no tengo miedo	I'm not afraid
no tengo ningún miedo	I'm not at all afraid
no tengo miedo alguno/no tengo nada de miedo	I'm not the slightest bit afraid

Note also the following:

no tengo ni idea/ni la menor idea/la más mínima idea
I haven't the slightest idea

7 Emphasising the negative (adjectives)

In the case of an adjective, the negative can be emphasised by placing nada before the adjective. Nada is invariable:

no encuentro sus libros nada interesantes
I don't find his books at all interesting

8 Emphasising the negative (verbs)

Nada can also be used as an emphatic negative rather than meaning 'nothing', though this construction is seldom used if the verb takes a direct object:

> **la película no me gustó nada**   **no he dormido nada**
> I didn't like the film at all   I haven't slept at all

If the verb has an object, a phrase such as en absoluto may be used:

> **no entiendo esto en absoluto**
> I don't understand this at all

Note that, on its own, en absoluto means '*not* at all':

> **¿me crees? – en absoluto**
> do you believe me? – not at all

E ASKING QUESTIONS

As was the case with negations, questions are formed using the standard or progressive forms of the verb, as appropriate.

1 Simple questions

Simple questions do not begin with an interrogative word. They can have the subject after the verb as in English:

> **¿está aquí tu hermano?**
> is your brother here?

However, they can sometimes be identical in form to statements, though this tends to suggest that the speaker expects the answer sí. In this case, the fact that they are questions is conveyed to the listener by the speaker's tone of voice:

> **¿el agua está fría?**
> is the water cold?

The idea of 'isn't it?' *etc* is expressed in Spanish by ¿no es verdad?,

¿verdad?, or more colloquially, simply ¿no?. These expressions
are all invariable:

> **tú le diste el dinero, ¿verdad?**
> you gave him the money, didn't you?

> **éste está mejor, ¿no es verdad?**   **te gusta hablar español, ¿no?**
> this one's better, isn't it?   you like speaking Spanish,
>   don't you?

2 Interrogative pronouns and adjectives

> ### Note
>
> Note that a preposition can *never* be placed at the end of a question
> in Spanish. Any preposition present must be placed in front of
> the interrogative pronoun or adjective. A Spanish speaker will not
> connect a preposition placed anywhere else in the question with
> the interrogative word, and will consequently not understand the
> question:
>
> **¿a quién le diste el dinero?**
> who did you give the money to? (to whom did you give the money?)
>
> **¿con quién fuiste al cine?**
> who did you go to the cinema with?

Note that cuál is an interrogative pronoun. If the noun is expressed,
cuál must be followed by de:

> **¿cuál de los coches prefieres?**   **¿cuál te gustó más?**
> which of the cars do you prefer?   which did you like best?

Qué is used (1) as an indefinite interrogative pronoun or (2) as an
interrogative adjective immediately in front of a noun:

> **¿qué quieres?**   **¿qué libro te gustó más?**
> what do you want?   which book did you like most?

Note that qué is invariable.

3 Indirect questions

Indirect questions are introduced either by the conjunction si (whether), or by an interrogative pronoun or adjective. The tenses used are identical to those used in English:

> **me preguntó si había visto la película**
> he asked me if I had seen the film

> **no sé cuál de los coches prefiero**
> I don't know which of the cars I prefer

Again, any preposition *must* precede the pronoun or adjective:

> **se negó a decirme con quién había salido**
> he refused to tell me who he had gone out with

F REFLEXIVE USES OF THE VERB

1 The reflexive pronouns

A verb is used reflexively if the subject of the verb performs the action on himself/herself/itself. The verb is made reflexive in Spanish by using it with the appropriate form of the reflexive pronoun (*see* page 203).

In English, a number of verbs can be used either with or without the reflexive pronoun without changing their meaning. For example, there is no real difference between 'I wash' and 'I wash myself', between 'he shaves' and 'he shaves himself'. This freedom to choose is not available in Spanish. If a particular action is perceived as reflexive, the reflexive forms of the verb *must* be used.

The number of actions which are perceived as reflexive is much greater in Spanish than in English:

> **se levantó, se lavó, se vistió y salió**
> he got up, got washed, got dressed and went out

The indirect reflexive pronouns express the idea of 'for oneself':

> **se compró un disco**
> he bought himself an album

Note

The reflexive pronouns are also essential with actions done to parts of one's own body or one's own clothes. Where English would use the possessive adjective, the noun is preceded by the *definite article* in Spanish:

se rompió la pierna
he broke his leg

se puso la chaqueta
he put on his jacket

2 The prefix auto-

In contemporary Spanish a number of reflexive verbs also have the prefix auto- (meaning 'self') joined to them to emphasise the reflexive nature of the action. However, such verbs should be used with care. Use only those you have seen and know to exist:

se autoexcluyeron
they opted out (they excluded themselves)

estos grupos se autoubican en la izquierda
these groups claim to be (place themselves) on the left

This prefix is also found in a large number of nouns: autodominio (self-control), autocrítica (self-criticism) *etc*.

3 Reciprocal action

A verb can be used reflexively not only to express the idea of doing an action to oneself, but also to express the idea of doing the action 'to each other'. In such cases the verb is invariably plural:

nos encontramos en la calle
we met each other in the street

nos vemos mañana
see you tomorrow
(= we'll see each other tomorrow)

If the verb is itself reflexive, the reciprocal action may be indicated by the use of uno a otro, though this also may be omitted if the context makes it clear that reciprocal action is involved.

se felicitaron uno a otro
they congratulated each other

If the verb takes a preposition before its object, this preposition will replace the a of uno a otro:

se despidieron uno de otro
they said goodbye to each other

Se despidieron would simply mean 'they said goodbye'.

In very formal language, uno a otro can be replaced by the adverbs mútuamente or recíprocamente:

se ayudan mútuamente
they help each other

4 Other meanings

A number of verbs can be used reflexively in Spanish with little or no true reflexive meaning, and with very little difference in meaning from the non-reflexive forms. The commonest of these are:

caer, caerse	to fall
morir, morirse	to die

Others change their meanings in largely unpredictable ways:

comer	to eat	comerse	to eat up
dormir	to sleep	dormirse	to go to sleep
ir	to go	irse	to go away
llevar	to carry	llevarse	to take away
quedar	to remain, to be left	quedarse	to stay

G GIVING COMMANDS

For the formation of the imperative, see pages 231-3. *For the position of pronouns with imperatives, see* pages 204-5.

It is important to remember that the imperative proper is used only for positive commands addressed either to tú or vosotros/vosotras.

In *all* other cases (positive commands addressed to **Vd.** and **Vds.**, and *all* negative commands) the appropriate form of the subjunctive is used:

> **no leas esa revista, lee ésta**
> don't read that magazine, read this one

> **tenéis que escribir la carta en español, no la escribáis en inglés**
> you have to write the letter in Spanish, don't write it in English

> **vengan mañana, no vengan hoy**
> come tomorrow, don't come today

The subjunctive is also used for third person imperatives, which are usually preceded by **que**:

> **¡qué lo hagan ellos mismos!**
> let them do it themselves!

First person imperatives (ie 'we') may be formed either by the subjunctive, or by **vamos a** followed by the infinitive of the verb. The use of the subjunctive implies a more committed attitude to the action in question:

> **vamos a ver**
> let's see

> **vamos a empezar**
> let's start

> **hagamos eso ahora mismo**
> let's do it right now

H THE PASSIVE

1 ser + past participle

The passive is formed in Spanish by **ser** plus the past participle. It must be borne clearly in mind that the passive is used exclusively to express an *action*. If you are not referring to an action but are describing a state, then **estar** will be used.

In this construction the past participle *always* agrees with the subject, ie with the thing or person to whom the action was done:

el palacio fue construido en el siglo XV
the palace was built in the 15th century

This is a reference to the castle actually being built. Compare also the following:

la ventana fue rota por la explosión
the window was shattered by the explosion

cuando entré en la sala vi que la ventana estaba rota
when I went into the room I saw that the window was broken

The first of these sentences refers to an action which occurred at a precise moment in time. The second describes a state. The corresponding action took place some time before you entered the room – you are now describing the *state* the window was in when you entered the room.

> ## Note
>
> The construction **ser** + past participle cannot be used to express the idea of 'to' or 'for' as in English – there is no direct Spanish equivalent of 'I was given a book' (a book was given *to* me). If you have to express such an idea in Spanish, a different construction must be used (see opposite).

2 Use of the reflexive

An alternative method of expressing the passive in Spanish is to put the verb into the reflexive form. This is not a way of 'avoiding' the passive. On the contrary, this construction is interpreted as a genuine passive by Spaniards. On hearing the sentence:

el palacio se construyó en 1495
the palace was built in 1495

no Spaniard believes, even for the merest fraction of a second, that the palace actually built itself.

> **se dice con frecuencia que España es un país atrasado**
> it is often said that Spain is an underdeveloped country

> **las mercancías pueden mandarse por vía aérea**
> the goods can be sent by air freight

This construction can be used to express the idea of 'to' or 'for' by combining it with the appropriate form of the indirect object pronoun. However, this is very formal, and the construction using the third person plural of the active form would normally be preferred:

> **se me concedió un libro como premio**
> **me concedieron un libro como premio**
> I was given a book as a prize

3 Use of the active forms of the verb

Although by no means rare, the passive forms are rather less used in Spanish than in English. It is always possible to use the active forms of the verb instead, and indeed this construction is necessary in certain circumstances. For example, 'I was given a book by the teacher' must be expressed in Spanish as **el profesor me dio un libro**.

> **el vendedor me ofreció un descuento del diez por ciento**
> I was offered a ten per cent discount by the salesman

If no agent is expressed, the third person plural form of the verb is used:

> **construyeron la central hace dos años**
> the power station was built two years ago

> **suprimirán todos los derechos de aduana**
> all customs duties will be abolished

5 SITUATING ACTIONS IN TIME

A EXPRESSING TIME THROUGH VERBAL PHRASES

Verbal phrases of time are extremely useful in that they can be applied to any time, present, past or future, without any change in their form.

1 Preposition + infinitive

a) Prepositions of time + infinitive

Most verbal phrases of time are formed by a preposition of time followed by a verb in the infinitive. This construction is most often used when the subject of the infinitive is the same as the subject of the main verb of the sentence:

tomé un café antes de salir
I had a coffee before leaving

después de terminar mis deberes, escucharé la radio
after finishing my homework, I'll listen to the radio

In rather literary style, it is possible for the infinitive to have a different subject from the main verb, but this subject must be placed *after* the infinitive:

me cambié de ropa antes de llegar mis amigos
I changed before my friends arrived

b) al + infinitive

This is a very useful construction in Spanish, though it is more common in the written than in the spoken language. The closest

English equivalent is 'on' + present participle. It expresses simultaneous actions in present, future or past time. It may even take its own subject which can be different from that of the main verb in the sentence:

al entrar vieron los otros salir
when they came in (on coming in) they saw the others leaving

al aparecer el cantante, el público aplaudió
when the singer appeared, the audience applauded

This construction can also have a causal meaning:

al tratarse de una emergencia, llamamos a un médico
since it was an emergency, we called a doctor

2 Preposition + past participle

In literary Spanish, both **después de** and **una vez** can be used with the past participle to form a phrase of time, though this construction is never used in the spoken language. The past participle agrees with the subject of the phrase:

después de terminadas las clases, volvimos a casa
after classes had finished we returned home

pagaremos la factura una vez entregadas las mercancías
we shall pay the invoice once the goods have been delivered

B EXPRESSING PRESENT TIME

1 The use of the progressive forms of the present tense

The progressive forms consist of the appropriate form of estar (*see* pages 107, 248) followed by the present participle of the verb (verbs other than estar may also be used, as explained below). The use of the progressive forms in Spanish is by and large similar to their use in English, though they are less common in Spanish.

a) **estar + present participle**

The progressive forms present any action essentially as an *activity*. If something cannot be viewed as an activity, the progressive forms are not used in Spanish, for example:

me siento bien
I feel fine/I'm feeling fine

The progressive forms are used for an action which is seen as actually taking place:

no hagas tanto ruido, estoy escuchando la radio
don't make so much noise, I'm listening to the radio (I'm listening to it right now)

They are also used when an activity was begun in the past and the speaker still feels involved in it, even though it may not actually be happening right now:

estoy escribiendo una tesis sobre la política española
I'm writing a thesis on Spanish politics

I may not be writing it at this very minute (in fact, I may not have worked on it for several weeks), but I've already started and it's one of my current activities.

Compare:

no me interrumpas, estoy pensando
don't interrupt me, I'm thinking

and

pienso que tienes razón
I think you're right

In the first sentence, 'thinking' is seen as an activity, in the second it is not.

Unlike English, the progressive forms in Spanish cannot be used to express intentions or to refer to future time. In such cases the standard present must be used:

vamos a España la semana que viene
we are going to Spain next week

They are also rather less widely used in questions and negative statements than their English counterparts:

¿por qué me miras así?
why are you looking at me like that?

no estudio griego
I'm not studying Greek

However, they can be used in such constructions if the idea of activity is to be emphasised:

no está cantando, está gritando
he isn't singing, he's shouting

b) ir + present participle

This construction emphasises the gradual nature of an action, and also suggests its continuation into the future:

poco a poco nos vamos acostumbrando
we are slowly getting used to it (and will continue to do so)

la tasa de inflación va aumentando
the rate of inflation is rising (and will continue to rise)

c) venir + present participle

Venir indicates that the action has continued from the past to the present. In fact, it points so clearly towards the past that it is often translated into English not by a present tense, but by a perfect tense:

las medidas que vienen adoptando son inútiles
the measures they have been adopting are pointless

los ejercicios que venimos haciendo no son interesantes
the exercises we've been doing aren't interesting

2 The general present

All other aspects of present time (repeated actions, general truths, and the like) are expressed by the standard forms of the present tense:

vamos a España todos los años   **la vida es dura**
we go to Spain every year   life is difficult

C FUTURE TIME IN A MAIN CLAUSE

1 The committed and uncommitted future

Spanish differentiates between a committed future and an uncommitted future, and can also express a completed future. All of these variations on future time can also be expressed as futures in the past.

The committed future is expressed in Spanish by the *present* tense of the verb. The uncommitted future is expressed by the standard future tense. Note however that the present tense can only be used to refer to the future if there is some other word in the sentence which points clearly to future time or if the context clearly relates to the future.

The present tense can also be used to express a committed future in English (eg 'I'm leaving tomorrow', 'the ship sails next Tuesday'), but its use is less widespread than it is in Spanish.

a) Present and future tenses

It must be stressed that the difference between these two futures is in no way related to the action being referred to, or to its distance from the speaker in time. It is quite possible to use both futures in relation to the same action. What determines the speaker's choice is his level of commitment to the action to which he is referring.

Compare the following:
lo hago mañana
lo haré mañana

Both of these mean 'I will do it tomorrow'. However, the first expresses a much more solid intention on the part of the speaker to actually do it.

The committed future is rather more common in the first person singular and plural ('I' and 'we').

However, it is also used with the third persons if the speaker is referring to an event about which he is absolutely certain:

los Reyes visitan Alemania la semana que viene
the King and Queen are visiting (will visit) Germany next week

el primer centenario de la democracia se celebra en 2077
the first centenary of democracy will take place in 2077

Both of these sentences could have been written using the future tense (visitarán and celebrará), but the speaker would in this way have indicated a certain remoteness from the event.

The present tense is also widely used in direct requests for immediate action:

¿me prestas veinte euros?
will you lend me twenty euros?

A less direct alternative is to use the verbs poder or querer followed by the infinitive:

¿puedes darme esas tijeras?
will you give me that pair of scissors?

¿quieres pasarme ese bolígrafo?
will you pass me that pen?

The use of the future tense in a request indicates that an immediate response is not being asked for:

¿me terminarás eso?
will you finish that for me?
(at some point in the future)

b) ir a + infinitive

As in the English construction 'I am going to do that later', a committed future can also be expressed in Spanish using ir a followed by the infinitive, though it is rather less common than its English equivalent:

voy a estudiar medicina en la universidad
I am going to study medicine at university

van a ver esa película mañana
they're going to see that film tomorrow

> ## Note
>
> An apparent future in English is sometimes not an expression of future time, but of willingness or refusal. Such ideas are expressed by the verbs querer, negarse or similar in Spanish:
>
> **se niega a tomar el desayuno por la mañana**
> he won't eat his breakfast in the morning
>
> **no quiere aceptar las reglas**
> he won't accept the rules

2 The completed future

The completed future is used to relate one action in the future to another action. It indicates that the action in question will have been completed by the time the second action applies. In a main clause, the completed future is expressed by the future perfect tense (*for formation see page 227*):

ya lo habré hecho cuando vuelvas
I'll already have done it when you come back

si llegamos tarde, ya se habrá marchado
if we arrive late he'll already have gone

It can also be used to indicate that the action will have been completed before a particular moment in time:

ya habrá venido
he will already have arrived

lo habré terminado para sábado
I will have finished it by Saturday

3 Future in the past

The following sentence gives an example of future in the past:

> **me dijo que iba a España la semana siguiente**
> he told me he was going to Spain the following week

He said **voy a España**, referring to the future. However, he said this in the past, so this is a case of future in the past.

In a main clause, future in the past is expressed either by the imperfect (committed future) or by the conditional (uncommitted future). However, the conditional is considerably more common in this construction than the imperfect:

> **me explicó que lo haría después de volver de sus vacaciones**
> he told me he would do it when he came back from his holidays

The conditional perfect expresses completed future in the past:

> **me aseguró que habría terminado el trabajo antes de medianoche**
> he assured me that he would have finished the work by midnight

D THE FUTURE IN SUBORDINATE CLAUSES OF TIME

A subordinate clause of time is a clause which is introduced by a word or phrase of time such as **cuando, así que, antes de que** and the like.

> Note
>
> In a subordinate clause of time, future time is expressed by the appropriate tense of the subjunctive of the verb.

1 The future

The future is expressed by the present subjunctive. There is no distinction between a committed and an uncommitted future:

> **en cuanto llegue, se lo diré**
> as soon as he arrives, I will tell him

¿qué harás cuando termine tu contrato?
what will you do when your contract runs out?

Note that after the conjunctions mientras and hasta que, both
meaning 'until', the word no is sometimes placed before the verb in
the subordinate clause. It must be kept in mind that this does *not*
make the verb negative. It is simply a quirk of style and does not
affect the verb in any way:

no podemos hacerlo mientras no nos autoricen
we can't do it until they authorise us

**no podemos mandar las mercancías hasta que no nos manden el
    pedido**
we can't send the goods until they send us the order

2 The completed future

In a subordinate clause of time, the completed future is expressed
by the perfect subjunctive:

podrás salir cuando hayas terminado tus deberes
you will be able to go out when you've finished your homework

insisto en que te quedes hasta que lo hayas hecho
I insist that you stay until you have done it

3 Future in the past

In a subordinate clause of time, future in the past is expressed by
the imperfect subjunctive:

me aseguró que lo haría en cuanto llegara
he assured me that he would do it as soon as he arrived

nos informaron que los mandarían tan pronto como fuese posible
they informed us they would send them as soon as possible

E PAST TIME

Spanish distinguishes between four levels of past time. These are:

past related to the present	*expressed by*	the perfect tense
the past in progress	*expressed by*	the imperfect tense
the completed past	*expressed by*	the preterite tense
the more distant past	*expressed by*	the pluperfect tense

Note that the tense you choose is not dependent in any sense on the action to which you are referring. It is not dependent on the nature of the action (ie whether it is a single action or a repeated action), nor on the duration of the action (whether it lasted one second or a century), nor on its position in time (whether it happened a minute ago or a thousand years ago).

The tense you choose is determined *entirely* by your subjective perception of the action, particularly as regards its relation to present time and its relation to other actions to which you also refer.

1 Past related to the present

The perfect tense is used to refer to a past action which, though completed, the speaker sees as somehow related to the present. The relationship seen between the past action and present time is often indicated by the presence of related verbs or adverbs referring to present time. There is no limit to how long ago the action or series of actions may have taken place.

By and large, the uses of the perfect tense in Spanish and English coincide (*but see* SPECIAL CASES, page 91):

he visitado a muchos países europeos últimamente
I have visited many European countries recently

en los últimos diez años he aprendido cuatro idiomas extranjeros
in the last ten years I have learned four foreign languages

2 The past in progress

The past in progress is expressed by the imperfect tense. An action
will be expressed in the imperfect tense if what is uppermost in
the speaker's mind is the fact that the action was in progress as
opposed to having been completed. There is no limit to how short
or long the action can be.

As a rule, the imperfect is used in Spanish where English would use
the imperfect progressive forms ('I was talking', 'he was writing'
etc), or forms such as 'I used to talk', and the like:

cuando era pequeño, iba todos los días a la piscina
when I was little, I went (used to go) to the swiming pool
every day

mientras Pepe veía la televisión, Juan hacía sus deberes
while Pepe was watching TV, Juan was doing his homework

Note

In particular, if one action is presented as occurring while another
is already in progress, the action 'occurring' will be expressed by
the *preterite*, and the action in progress by the *imperfect*:

mientras Juan llamaba a la puerta, el teléfono sonó
while Juan was knocking on the door, the telephone rang

Like the present tense, the imperfect also has a progressive form,
formed by the imperfect of estar plus the present participle of the
verb. This again presents the action primarily as an activity:

estábamos escuchando la radio cuando María entró
we were listening to the radio when María came in

Note

An apparent conditional in English is not always a genuine conditional. In a sentence such as 'he would always read his paper on the train', the 'would' is used to highlight the fact that the action is seen extending over time. This is translated by the *imperfect* in Spanish:

siempre leía su periódico en el tren
he would always read his paper on the train

3 The completed past

The completed past indicates that the aspect of the action (or series of actions) which is most important for the speaker is the fact that it has been completed. Whether the action was a repeated one, or whether it lasted a great length of time is unimportant. If completion is being stressed, the preterite will be used:

hizo esto cada día durante casi diez años
he did this every day for almost ten years

viví en España durante más de veinte años
I lived in Spain for over twenty years

It should be possible from these examples to see that it is perfectly feasible in Spanish to use either the imperfect or the preterite to refer to the same action, depending on how your subjective perception of the action changes. The following small narrative should illustrate the point:

Juan llamó a la puerta. Mientras llamaba a la puerta, el teléfono sonó. Mientras el teléfono sonaba, el bebé empezó a llorar.
Juan knocked at the door. While he was knocking at the door, the telephone rang. While the telephone was ringing, the baby started to cry.

4 Stylistic expressions of past time

a) Present for preterite

For reasons of style, past time is often expressed, particularly in written Spanish, by the present tense of the verb (the so-called historic present). This is used to lend a dramatic quality to a narrative. The historic present is also used in English, though to a lesser extent than in Spanish:

en el siglo XV sale Colón para América
in the 15th century Columbus set sail for America

It would also have been possible to use the present tense in English here.

b) Imperfect for preterite

Again in written Spanish, and once more for reasons of style and dramatic effect, an action is sometimes expressed in the imperfect where a preterite would have been the everyday choice:

en 1975 moría Franco y comenzaba la transición a la democracia
in 1975 Franco died and the transition to democracy began

5 The more distant past

a) Pluperfect

The more distant past is expressed by the pluperfect. An action belongs to the more distant past if the speaker wishes to indicate that it was completed *before* another action in the past:

llegué a las tres, pero Juan ya se había marchado
I got there at three, but Juan had already gone

no podía salir porque había perdido su llave
he couldn't go out because he had lost his key

b) Past anterior

In very literary Spanish, the more distant past in a subordinate clause of time is sometimes expressed by the past anterior:

cuando hubimos terminado, nos marchamos
when we had finished, we left

The past anterior is not used in spoken Spanish, and would give a distinctly literary flavour in contemporary written Spanish. The pluperfect or the simple preterite are usually used instead.

F SPECIAL CASES

1 Actions on the limits of present and past time

a) The future limit

Actions which are about to take place are expressed in Spanish by the present tense of estar a punto de or less commonly estar para followed by the infinitive:

estoy a punto de empezar   **el tren está para salir**
I'm just about to start   the train is just about to leave

The imperfect is used when this idea is expressed in the past:

estaba a punto de salir cuando Juan llegó
I was just about to go out when Juan arrived

b) The past limit

Actions which have just taken place are expressed by the present tense of acabar de followed by the infinitive:

acabamos de ver el programa
we have just seen the programme

acaban de volver del cine
they've just come back from the cinema

Again, the imperfect is used if this idea is expressed in the past:

acabábamos de poner la tele cuando entraron
we had just switched on the telly when they came in

2 Actions continuing from one time to another

An action which starts in the past and continues right up to the present (and may well continue into the future) is considered in Spanish to belong to present time, and is therefore expressed by the present tense.

a) Present tense + desde (hace)

The length of time involved is introduced by desde if a starting point is indicated, or by desde hace if a length of time is stated. This is in complete contrast with English which uses the perfect tense with 'for':

¿desde cuándo esperas aquí?
how long have you been waiting here for?

espero aquí desde hace casi media hora
I've been waiting here for almost half an hour

estudio español desde 2004
I've been studying Spanish since 2004

estudio español desde hace dos años
I've been studying Spanish for two years

b) hace + present tense + que

Alternatively, the time span can be introduced by hace followed by a subordinate clause introduced by que:

hace media hora que espero aquí
I've been waiting here for half an hour

c) llevar + present participle

A further possibility is to use the present tense of the verb llevar followed by the present participle of the verb:

llevamos tres meses aprendiendo el ruso
we've been learning Russian for three months

d) Continuing actions in the past

When these actions are expressed in the past, all the constructions given above are used in the imperfect (as opposed to the pluperfect in English):

trabajaba desde hacía diez años como profesor
he had been working as a teacher for ten years

hacía veinte años que vivían en España
they'd been living in Spain for twenty years

llevaba quince minutos esperando
I had been waiting for fifteen minutes

6 DESCRIBING AN ACTION

A THE ADVERB

For the formation of adverbs, see page 208.

> ### Note
>
> It is essential to remember that adverbs are invariable – they never change their form whatever the circumstances in which they are used:
>
> **entraron lenta y silenciosamente**
> they came in slowly and quietly
>
> **tú trabajas mucho más rápidamente que yo**
> you work much more quickly than I do

1 Adverbial phrases

Rather than a simple adverb, Spanish very often uses adverbial phrases formed mostly with the nouns manera or modo:

   esto nos afecta de una manera indirecta
   this affects us indirectly

Noun/adjective combinations may also be used:

   hablar en alta voz/en voz baja
   to speak loudly/quietly

2 The use of adjectives

An attractive feature of Spanish is its ability to use adjectives with almost adverbial force. In this case the adjectives must agree with the *subject* of the verb:

   vivieron felices durante muchos años
   they lived happily for many years

le miramos atónitos
we looked at him in astonishment

B VARYING THE FORCE OF AN ADVERB

1 Another adverb

As in English, one adverb may be used to vary the force of another:

lo hizo increíblemente bien
he did it unbelievably well

Adverbs of time and place can be emphasised by adding mismo after them; mismo is invariable in this usage:

aquí mismo, ahora mismo
right here, right now

2 Comparative and superlative

The comparative and superlative of adverbs are formed in exactly the same way as those of adjectives (*see* pages 187-9).

tú trabajas más rápidamente que yo
you work more quickly than I do

However, when a phrase of possibility is placed after a superlative, lo is always placed before más (this construction is rarely translated by a superlative in English):

lo hicimos lo más rápidamente posible
we did it as quickly as possible

7 RELATIONSHIPS BETWEEN ACTIONS

A THE PRESENT PARTICIPLE

For the formation of the present participle, see **page 224.**

a) Expressing means

Only the present participle can be used in Spanish to express the idea of 'by doing', 'by going' and the like. No other construction is available:

gané este dinero trabajando durante las vacaciones
I earned this money by working during the holidays

conseguí hacerlo dejando otras cosas para más tarde
I managed to do it by leaving other things till later

> Note
>
> The Spanish word por can never be followed by a present participle. When followed by an infinitive, por does not express means, but *cause*:
>
> **le sirvieron primero por ser cliente regular**
> they served him first because he was a regular customer

b) Expressing simultaneous action

The present participle is widely used to express an action taking place simultaneously with another:

entró corriendo　　　　　　　　**'está bien', dijo sonriendo**
he rushed in　　　　　　　　　　　'OK', he said smiling
　(= he came in running)

This construction is often the only way of expressing certain phrasal verbs of motion in English (see 'he rushed in' above):

pasó corriendo
he ran past

> ## Note
>
> The present participle is invariable in Spanish, in other words it *never* changes its form, irrespective of the gender or number of the subject of the verb:
>
> **las chicas salieron corriendo**
> the girls rushed out
>
> After a verb of perception (seeing, hearing *etc*), the present participle may be replaced by an infinitive. In fact this construction is, if anything, more common than the use of the present participle:
>
> **vi a mi hermano atravesando/atravesar la calle**
> I saw my brother crossing the street

c) Cause

A present participle can also express cause:

estando en Madrid, decidí visitar a mi amigo
since I was in Madrid, I decided to call on my friend

no sabiendo como continuar, decidió pedir ayuda
not knowing how to proceed, he decided to ask for help

d) Continuation

The present participle is used with the verbs seguir and (less frequently) continuar to express the continuation of an action:

siguió trabajando a pesar de todo
he went on working in spite of everything

continuaron repitiendo la misma cosa
they kept on repeating the same thing

B INFINITIVE OR SUBORDINATE CLAUSE?

When two verbs are linked in Spanish, you must choose whether to put the second verb into the infinitive form (preceded or not by a preposition) or whether to put it into a subordinate clause introduced by que.

If the subject of both verbs is the same, in most cases you can use the simple infinitive. If the subjects are different, you must, with very few exceptions, put the second verb into a subordinate clause (and frequently also into the subjunctive). Compare:

1 Same subject

> **quiero hacerlo**
> I want to do it

I am not only the person 'wanting', I am also the person who wants 'to do' it. No-one else is involved.

> **entré sin verle**
> I came in without seeing him

I came in, and *I* did not see him.

Spanish goes further in the use of this construction than English does:

> **creyó estar soñando**
> he thought he was dreaming

> **creemos poder hacerlo**
> we think we can do it

2 Different subjects

Compare the sentences given above with:

> **quiero que tú lo hagas**
> I want you to do it

There are two people involved here. *I* 'want', but *you* are the person who is 'to do'.

entré sin que él me viera
I came in without him seeing me

I came in, but *he* did not see me.

3 Verbs where the infinitive may take a different subject

There are a small number of verbs with which the subject of a following infinitive may be different from that of the first verb (*see* **page 259**):

me dejaron entrar
they let me come in

4 Infinitives after prepositions

The most obvious exceptions to the general 'rule' are phrases consisting of a preposition followed by an infinitive. In this case the infinitive may have a subject which is different from that of the main verb, but this subject is always placed *after* the infinitive:

quiero hacerlo antes de llegar los otros
I want to do it before the others arrive

However, such expressions are rather literary in style, and even in these cases Spaniards will often prefer to use a subordinate clause:

quiero hacerlo antes de que lleguen los otros
I want to do it before the others arrive

C THE INFINITIVE

1 Verb + preposition + infinitive

A verb used in the infinitive after another verb can either appear on its own, or can be introduced by one of a wide range of prepositions. There are few truly useful rules for predicting which preposition is to be used, and in most cases the preposition required must simply be learned through observation and practice.

For a list of the prepositions required by some common verbs, see pages 254-7.

2 Adjective + infinitive

It may be useful at this point to note the following very common construction in Spanish:

(indirect object +) verb + adjective + infinitive

The indirect object may be a pronoun or a noun. The verb may be ser, parecer, resultar or similar. A wide range of adjectives is available and any verb can be used in the infinitive after the adjective:

me es difícil creer lo que estás diciendo
it's difficult for me to believe what you're saying

nos parece absurdo proponer tal cosa
it seems absurd to us to suggest such a thing

The same construction can be used with various verbs of 'considering', but in this case there is no indirect object:

encuentro difícil aceptar esto
I find it difficult to accept this

consideramos poco aconsejable continuar así
we consider it inadvisable to continue in this way

3 Adjective + de + infinitive

If the adjective is not part of an impersonal expression, but relates to an identifiable thing or things already stated in the sentence, it is then followed by de + infinitive. The adjective agrees with the thing being described:

estos ejercicios son fáciles de hacer
these exercises are easy to do

encuentro este libro difícil de leer
I find this book difficult to read

4 que + infinitive

Note that que is placed before the infinitive in expressions such as the following:

tengo una factura que pagar
I've got a bill to pay

nos queda mucho trabajo que hacer
we still have lots of work to do

D THE SUBORDINATE CLAUSE: INDICATIVE OR SUBJUNCTIVE?

The verb in a subordinate clause will be either in the indicative or in the subjunctive. Since the subjunctive has all but disappeared in English, this can be a difficult concept for the learner of Spanish to grasp.

However, the subjunctive is very widely used in Spanish, and there is really little point in learning 'ways to avoid the subjunctive'. The best approach is to try to understand what the indicative and the subjunctive are used to express.

In general terms the indicative is used to introduce actions which the speaker *believes* to be clear and material statements of fact. The subjunctive, on the other hand, is used if the speaker feels that the statements are untrue, or if he feels unable in some way to guarantee that they will prove to be true, or if, rather than simply stating them, he is expressing an emotional reaction to them. This can be due to a variety of reasons, for example because:

- he doubts, disbelieves or denies the statements;
- the actions have not yet taken place: they belong to the future and therefore cannot be guaranteed;
- the actions are expressed as conditions which are not or cannot be fulfilled;
- the actions are introduced by a statement of emotion.

It is important to realise that there is no single set of rules for the use of the subjunctive in Spanish. For example, different rules apply when referring to future time than when expressing a condition or expressing emotion, and so on. Each case must be dealt with independently.

In general, however, *any* impersonal expression which does not introduce a straightforward statement of fact will be followed by the subjunctive:

> **es posible/probable/una pena que esté allí**
> it's possible/probable/a shame that he'll be there

 E INDIRECT OR REPORTED SPEECH

The indicative is used exclusively for statements and questions in indirect speech in Spanish, since the speaker is simply relating actions which he presents as having actually taken place. The tenses used in Spanish correspond exactly to those used in English.

Note

Contrary to English usage, *all* indirect statements must be introduced by que in Spanish. Omission of the word que would be confusing for your Spanish listener:

dijo que vendría más tarde
he said (that) he would come later

me explicó que ya lo habían hecho
he explained to me that they had already done it

le contesté que no sería posible
I replied that it wouldn't be possible

---

8 SOME SPECIAL VERBS

A TO BE

1 ser and estar

There are two verbs 'to be' in Spanish, ser and estar. In general terms it can be said that:

- ser is used to *define* things;
- estar is used to describe characteristics which could change without affecting the essential definition of the thing.

It is not necessarily the case that ser describes characteristics which are permanent and estar does not. The question of *definition* is much more important in deciding which verb to use.

The uses of these verbs can be divided into three categories:

- cases where ser is obligatory;
- cases where estar is obligatory;
- cases where either is possible.

These can be summarized as follows:

a) Cases where ser is obligatory

   i) When the verb 'to be' is followed by a noun, ser must be used, since a noun always provides at least a partial definition of the object in question.

   Typical examples would include professions, nationality or origin, names, statements of possession, materials from which something is made, expressions of time and almost all impersonal expressions:

   mi padre es minero
   my father is a miner

In Spanish, your occupation is considered to be at least part of your 'definition'. The fact that your father may lose his job one day and no longer be a miner (or that it may even be a temporary job) does not alter this in any way.

no somos portugueses, somos españoles
we are not Portuguese, we are Spaniards

España es un país interesante
Spain is an interesting country

Note that **es** goes with the noun **país** and not the adjective **interesante**. Your interest in Spain may diminish later, but it will continue to be a country.

este coche es de mi madre   **la mesa es de madera**
this car is my mother's   the table is made of wood

¿qué hora es? – son las dos de la tarde
what time is it? – it's two in the afternoon

es necesario hacerlo ahora mismo
it's necessary to do it right now

ii) **Ser** + adjectives describing defining characteristics

yo creo que el español es muy fácil de aprender
I think that Spanish is easy to learn

The fact that others might disagree, or that you might later change your mind, is irrelevant. For the time being 'easy' is part of your definition of Spanish.

Note that colour and size are usually considered to be defining characteristics in Spanish:

la plaza de toros es muy grande   **las paredes eran blancas**
the bull ring is very large   the walls were white

They may be painted a different colour later, but for the time being 'being white' is part of their definition.

If the colour is not seen as a defining characteristic, a different construction (and in some cases a different adjective) is likely to be used:

tenía los ojos enrojecidos
his eyes were red

iii) **Ser** is used with the past participle to express the passive in Spanish (*for an explanation of the passive, see* **pages 77-9**):

la cosecha fue destruida por las heladas
the crop was destroyed by the frosts

b) Cases where **estar** is obligatory

i) **Estar** must be used when referring to position, whether of persons or things, whether temporary or permanent. The position of an object, however permanent, is not seen as part of its definition in Spanish:

estuve en la playa ayer
I was at the beach yesterday

los pirineos están en la frontera entre España y Francia
the Pyrenees are on the frontier between Spain and France

They're likely to remain there for some time, but (in theory at least) the Pyrenees would still be the Pyrenees even if they turned up somewhere else.

Note that **estar** is used to express not only physical position, but also mental position and in fact position of any kind:

estamos a favor de las negociaciones
we are in favour of negotiations

estamos en contra de la política del gobierno
we are against the government's policy

el problem está en el precio
the problem is (lies in) the price

ii) **Estar** is used with the present participle of the verb to form the progressive forms in Spanish:

¿qué estás haciendo? – estoy leyendo una revista española
what are you doing? – I'm reading a Spanish magazine

estábamos escuchando la radio cuando Juan entró
we were listening to the radio when Juan came in

iii) **Estar** is typically used with adjectives to express moods and other temporary characteristics:

estoy furioso contigo
I'm furious with you

estoy muy cansado, he trabajado mucho hoy
I'm very tired, I've worked a lot today

'Being tired' is unlikely to be part of your definition. You will still be the same person when you have recovered your energy.

c) Cases where either is possible

When used with many other adjectives, either ser or estar may be possible. Which you choose will depend on the extent to which you feel that:

i) the adjective defines the thing in question, for however short a time this definition might apply, in which case you will use **ser**:

María es muy guapa
María is very pretty

ii) the adjective merely describes a characteristic of the thing in question, in which case you will use **estar**:

María está muy guapa hoy
María is looking very pretty today

Compare:

mi profesor es muy pesado   **estás muy pesado hoy**
my teacher is very boring   you're being a real bore today

eres tonto   **estás tonto**
you're silly   you're being silly

iii) In a negative command with adjectives like pesado and tonto, however, only ser would be used:

no seas tonto
don't be silly

Since silliness is not seen here as a mood in Spanish, estar cannot be used. With adjectives of mood, however, estar would be used:

no estés furioso
don't be furious

d) Some special cases

A few adjectives actually have different meanings when used with ser and estar:

	SER	ESTAR
bueno	good	well (*in good health*)
cansado	tiring (*person*)	tired
consciente	aware	conscious (*awake, not unconscious*)
grave	serious	seriously ill
listo	clever	ready
malo	bad	ill (*in poor health*)
moreno	dark-haired	suntanned
pesado	heavy (*thing*)	boring (*person*)
rico	rich	cute (*child*), nice (*food*)
seguro	sure (*thing*), safe (*thing*)	sure, certain (*person*)
verde	green	unripe

Other changes are more subtle. Compare ser viejo (to be old) with estar viejo (to look older than you are), ser pequeño (to be small) with estar pequeño (to be small for your age).

Note that, when referring to happiness, Spaniards invariably say estar contento, but both ser feliz and estar feliz are possible, depending on whether it refers to a defining characteristic or a mood.

2 encontrarse, hallarse, verse, quedar

Encontrarse and hallarse can sometimes replace estar:

el lago se encuentra detrás de la casa
the lake is behind the house

no me encuentro bien hoy
I don't feel well today

Both verse and quedar can replace ser when used with a past participle. Verse is almost always used in preference to ser with obligado:

el gobierno se vio obligado a retirar su propuesta
the government was forced to withdraw its proposal

la casa quedó completamente destruida
the house was completely destroyed

3 haber

'There is' and 'there are' are expressed in Spanish by hay. Hay is in fact the third person singular of the present tense of haber – ha – with the obsolete word y (there) tagged on at the end:

hay mucha gente en la playa
there are lots of people on the beach

It is important to realize that this is in fact part of the verb haber since it is the standard parts of haber which are used in all other tenses and constructions:

había por lo menos cincuenta personas en la habitación
there were at least fifty people in the room

Note that the singular form is always used, even when referring to a plural noun (personas). Note also the following infinitive construction:

debe haber otra manera de abordar el problema
there must be another way of approaching the problem

'There must be' is *never* debe ser or debe estar, which mean 'it must be'. However, in the following construction the appropriate forms of ser and estar are indeed used:

¿cuántos sois? – somos siete
how many of you are there? – there are seven of us

estábamos cinco en la cocina
there were five of us in the kitchen

4 deber

The phrases 'is to', 'was to' and the like, indicating that something is due to happen or was supposed to happen, are translated by the present or imperfect of deber:

> **el trabajo debía empezar el día cinco**
> work was to begin on the fifth

> **la factura debe pagarse a la entrega de las mercancías**
> the invoice is to be paid on delivery of the goods

5 General weather conditions

Most descriptions of general weather conditions are made using the verbs hacer and haber:

¿qué tiempo hace? what's the weather like?	**hace buen/mal tiempo** it's nice/bad weather
hace frío/calor it's cold/warm	**hace mucho sol** it's very sunny
hace/hay mucho viento it's very windy	**hay neblina** it's misty
había luna the moon was out	

Since Spanish uses nouns here as opposed to the English adjectives, the idea of 'very' is expressed by the appropriate form of mucho (or any other appropriate adjective or adjectival clause):

hace mucho calor it's very hot	**está haciendo un frío que pela** it's bitterly cold

Some weather conditions are expressed simply by a verb:

llueve/está lloviendo it's raining	**nieva/está nevando** it's snowing
hiela/está helando it's freezing	**tronaba/estaba tronando** it was thundering

6 Personal descriptions

Many personal descriptions are made using the verb tener:

tengo hambre/sed
I'm hungry/thirsty

tiene sueño/miedo
he's sleepy/scared

tenemos frío/calor
we're cold/hot

tengo ganas de ir
I'm keen to go

hemos tenido suerte
we were lucky

Again, since Spanish uses nouns here, 'very' is expressed by mucho or a similar adjective:

tenemos mucho frío
we are very cold

B TO BECOME

There is no single verb equivalent to 'to become' in Spanish. How you translate this idea will depend on its context:

a) 'become' with an adjective

With an adjective, 'become' is usually expressed by hacerse, ponerse or volverse. Ponerse indicates a temporary change, volverse indicates a longer-lasting one:

se puso furioso cuando oyó esta noticia
he became furious when he heard this piece of news

se hacía oscuro fuera
it was becoming dark outside

se volvió muy antipático
he became very unfriendly

b) 'become' with a noun

With a noun, 'become' is usually expressed by hacerse or convertirse en:

esta empresa se ha convertido en la más importante de España
this firm has become Spain's leading company

se hizo diputado a los 30 años de edad
he became an MP at the age of 30

If there is an idea of achievement, llegar a ser can also be used:

llegó a ser presidente a pesar de todas las dificultades
he became president despite all the difficulties

c) Other verbs

In many cases where the verb 'become' would be used in English, Spanish would choose a different approach altogether:

España ingresó en el Mercado Común en 1986
Spain became a member of the Common Market in 1986

C TO HAVE

1 tener and haber

a) tener

Tener expresses 'to have' in the sense of 'to possess':

¿tienes coche?
do you have a car?

¿cuánto dinero tienes?
how much money do you have?

Contar con and disponer de are also often used to express 'to have', less in the sense of 'to own' but 'to have at one's disposal':

este país cuenta con nueve centrales nucleares
this country has nine nuclear power stations

See also the following section.

b) haber

Haber is used with the participle to form the compound tenses of
verbs (*see* pages 226-7 *and* 230-1).

> ## Note
>
> In these constructions the past participle *never* changes its form,
> irrespective of the number and gender of either the subject or the
> object of the verb:
>
> **¿habéis visto la última película de Almodóvar?**
> have you seen Almodóvar's latest film?
>
> Visto is unaffected by the fact that habéis is plural (vosotros) or
> that película is feminine.

Tener is sometimes used with the participle to express an idea
similar to those of the compound tenses. This construction
cannot be used unless the verb has an object, and the past
participle agrees with the object of the verb:

ya tengo escritas las cartas
I have written the letters

The following two usages are particularly common:

tenemos pensado ir a jugar al tenis
we intend to go and play tennis

tengo entendido que ha sido un éxito
I understand it was a success

2 hacer

Note that phrases of the type 'to have a house built', 'to have the
room painted' *etc* are expressed in Spanish using the verb hacer. The
second verb goes into the infinitive, unlike English where the past
participle is used:

se hicieron construir una casa en el campo
they had a house built in the country

haremos ejecutar su pedido cuanto antes
we will have your order carried out as soon as possible

 D **TO KNOW**

There are two verbs 'to know' in Spanish, conocer and saber. Conocer means to know in the sense of 'to be familiar with', 'to be acquainted with'. Saber is to know in a mental or intellectual sense, to have learned or understood, to know something to be a fact. Compare the following:

¿conoces la teoría de la relatividad?
do you know the theory of relativity?

ie, have you heard of the theory of relativity? You may be able to answer sí to this question without having any idea what the theory means.

¿te sabes la teoría de la relatividad?
do you know the theory of relativity?

ie, do you understand the theory of relativity? Could you explain it?

Conocer is invariably used with people, countries and the like:

conozco muy bien a Pedro
I know Pedro very well

no conozco España
I don't know Spain
(I've never been there)

Saber is invariably used with noun clauses:

sé lo que estás pensando
I know what you're thinking

no sé como ocurrió esto
I don't know how this happened

 E **ACTIONS CONSIDERED IMPERSONAL IN SPANISH**

A number of commonly expressed actions take a personal subject in English, but are expressed by an impersonal construction in Spanish. As a result, what is considered to be the object of the verb in English becomes the subject of the Spanish verb, and it is with this subject that the verb agrees. The subject of the English verb is then expressed by an indirect object in Spanish.

The commonest of these verbs are:

verb	meaning	used to translate
faltar	to be absent	not to have enough of, to need, to be left
gustar	to please	to like
parecer	to seem	to think
quedar	to remain	to have ... left
sobrar	to exist in greater amounts than required	to have too much of, to have ... left

a) faltar

me faltan diez euros   **faltan dos horas**
I'm ten euros short   there are two hours left

The phrase hacer falta is also used with the same meaning:

me hace falta más tiempo
I need more time

b) gustar

Note

Always remember that gustar does not actually mean 'to like' – it means 'to please'. Consequently the English object becomes the Spanish subject, and the English subject becomes the Spanish indirect object. Gustar agrees in number with the thing 'liked':

a Juan no le gustan estos caramelos
Juan does not like these sweets (literally, the sweets are not pleasing to Juan)

nos gusta mucho la tortilla española
we like Spanish omelette very much

> Note—cont'd
>
> Although forms such as gusto or gustamos do occur, they are
> relatively infrequent. If you are tempted to use one of these forms,
> make sure you have not misunderstood how to use gustar.

If 'like' does not include the idea of 'please', gustar is not used:

quisiera más información sobre este hotel
I would like more information about this hotel

It is not that this information would be pleasing to you (it might
in fact be unpleasant). You are simply asking for information.

c) parecer

¿qué te parece mi nuevo coche? – me parece estupendo
what do you think of my new car? – I think it's great

esa idea me parece ridícula
I find that idea ridiculous

d) quedar

¿cuánto dinero te queda?
how much money do you have left?

nos quedaban dos horas
we had two hours left

e) sobrar

aquí sobran jefes y faltan guerreros
there are too many chiefs and not enough Indians

me sobran veinte euros   **nos sobra tiempo**
I have twenty euros left   we've got loads of time

Note also the phrase:

basta y sobra
there's more than enough

9 COMMUNICATING IN SPANISH

A BELIEF/DISBELIEF/DOUBT/DENIAL

Statements of belief in the positive, however vague, are followed
by the verb in the indicative *irrespective of whether the statement
is actually true in fact*. The fact that the statement is presented as
being true is sufficient to require the indicative to be used:

tenía la impresión de que ya te habías marchado
I was under the impression you'd already left

The fact that you're still here is irrelevant.

supongo que vendrá   **creo que tienes razón**
I suppose he'll come   I think you're right

Note that Spanish uses que in expressions such as the following:

creo que sí   **creo que no**
I think so   I don't think so

1 Direct questions

In the case of a direct question, either the indicative or the
subjunctive may be used. The subjunctive expresses actual doubt
on the part of the speaker. If the speaker is simply unsure, the
indicative is used. In usage the indicative is more common in this
construction than the subjunctive.

¿crees que Juan vendrá mañana?
do you think that Juan will come tomorrow?

¿crees que Juan venga?
do you think that Juan will come? (I suspect he won't)

2 Verbs of belief in the negative, or verbs of doubting or denying in the affirmative

If a verb of belief is used in the negative, or if a verb of doubting or denying is used in the affirmative, the verb in the subordinate clause is in the subjunctive:

> **no creo que sea justo decir eso**
> I don't think it's fair to say that
> **dudo que consiga hacerlo**
> I doubt that he'll manage to do it
> **niego absolutamente que sea así**
> I absolutely deny that this is the case

It is important to differentiate between statements of opinion and indirect speech. In the latter the indicative is *always* used whether the introductory verb is positive or negative. Compare:

> **yo no digo que el Gobierno tenga razón**
> I'm not saying that the Government is right
> **yo no dije que Juan había llegado**
> I didn't say that Juan had arrived

The first of these is a statement of opinion. The second is a narrative of events which happened (or did not happen) in the past.

3 Verbs of doubting or denying in the negative

If a verb of doubting or denying is used in the negative, either the subjunctive or the indicative may be used. The indicative is used if the speaker is very positive about what is being said:

> **no dudo que tengas/tienes razón**

The use of **tengas** implies something like 'I don't doubt that you might be right', whereas the use of **tienes** means 'I am quite sure that you are right'.

> **no niego que sea/es posible hacerlo**
> I don't deny that it might be/is possible to do it

B CONDITIONS

Conditions in Spanish can be divided into two large groups, each of which requires a different use of the verb:

Type	Definition	Verb
open-ended conditions	those which may or may not be fulfilled, those whose outcome has not yet been decided	indicative
unfulfilled conditions	those which are presented as unfulfilled, those which the speaker believes not to be the case or not to have been carried out	subjunctive

You must be clear which kind of condition you are dealing with, since the rules for expressing the different kinds of conditions are markedly different from each other.

If the condition is perceived as open-ended in the sense that it may or may not be fulfilled, the indicative is used (with one exception – see open-ended conditions of future time opposite):

si llueve mañana, iré al cine
if it rains tomorrow, I'll go to the cinema

If the condition is perceived as genuinely unreal in the sense that it has not been or cannot be fulfilled, the subjunctive is used in the si clause:

si fuera rico, no trabajaría
if I was rich, I wouldn't work

Do not confuse conditions with the conditional tenses. The *tenses* used in Spanish are in all cases identical to English. The differences between the two languages relate to the uses of the indicative and the subjunctive.

1 Open-ended conditions

Open-ended conditions in Spanish can relate to present, future or past time. They are expressed as follows:

a) Present time

Open-ended conditions relating to present time are expressed in Spanish by the present indicative. The verb in the main clause is usually in the present indicative or sometimes in the imperative:

si quieres evitar más problemas, cállate
if you want to avoid further problems, keep quiet

ie if you want to avoid problems *now*. You may choose either to avoid the problems or not.

si no te gusta éste, puedes tomar otro
if you don't like this one, you can take another

You may in fact like this one, in which case you won't take another.

b) Future time

Conditions relating to future time are by definition open-ended since their outcome cannot yet be known. Future conditions are expressed in Spanish by the present indicative. The verb in the main clause is usually future (committed or uncommitted):

si vuelves borracho, te mato
if you come home drunk I'll kill you

si no lo termino a tiempo, no podré salir
if I don't finish in time, I won't be able to go out

si lo haces, te doy mil euros
if you do it, I'll give you a thousand euros

> ## Note
>
> An open-ended condition of future time *may* take the imperfect subjunctive if the speaker wishes to present it as a more remote possibility. The conditional is then used in the main clause:
>
> **si hicieras eso, los otros se enfadarían**
> if you were to do that, the others would be annoyed
>
> This is a more remote condition than:
>
> **si haces eso, los otros se enfadarán**
> if you do that the others will be annoyed
>
> but both refer to future time.

c) Past time

Open-ended conditions relating to past time take the same tense of the verb as in English:

si no ha hecho sus deberes, no podrá salir
if he hasn't done his homework, he won't be able to go out

He may indeed have done it. You are expressing this condition precisely because you are unsure. The condition may indeed have been fulfilled.

si lo utilizó, sabrá como funciona
if he used it, he'll know how it works

You are unable to say for certain whether he used it or not.

si no llovía, ¿por qué estás mojado?
if it wasn't raining, why are you wet?

2 Unfulfilled conditions

Unfulfilled conditions relate only to present time and past time.

a) Present time

Unfulfilled conditions relating to present time are expressed in Spanish by the imperfect subjunctive. Either form of the imperfect subjunctive may be used. The verb in the main clause is usually, though not always, in the conditional:

si Juan estuviera aquí, hablaría con él
if Juan was here I'd speak to him

ie if he was here *now*. You would not be saying this unless you believed that he was *not* there. The fact that he might be there is irrelevant. In your opinion this is an unfulfilled condition.

si tuviera dinero, iría a España
if I had money, I'd go to Spain

si fuera más barato, lo compraríamos
if it was cheaper, we'd buy it

Again, you are only saying this because you do not believe you have enough money.

b) The completed past

Unfulfilled conditions relating to the completed past are expressed in Spanish by the pluperfect subjunctive (either the hubiera or the hubiese forms). They are unfulfilled in that they refer to events which did not in fact take place. The verb in the main clause is usually in the conditional perfect or less commonly in the pluperfect subjunctive (hubiera forms):

si lo hubiéramos sabido, habríamos venido
if we had known, we would have come

We didn't know, so we didn't come.

si hubieras llegado a tiempo, le habrías visto
if you'd arrived on time, you'd have seen him

3 como + present subjunctive

In colloquial Spanish, como + present subjunctive is frequently used to express a condition of future time. The subjunctive is *always* used in this construction even though the condition is open-ended:

como llegues tarde me enfado
if you arrive late I'll be angry

Como is not interchangeable with si in all cases. If you are unsure, it is always safer to use si.

4 de + infinitive

In formal written Spanish, a condition is sometimes expressed by the preposition de followed by the infinitive:

de continuar así, suspenderá el examen
if he goes on like this, he'll fail the exam

For past time the perfect infinitive is used:

de haberlo sabido, no habría venido
if I had known I wouldn't have come

5 Negative conditions

Any condition can be made negative by simply placing no before the verb in the conditional clause or by using some other negative:

si no haces tus deberes, no podrás salir
if you don't do your homework, you won't be able to go out

However, negative conditions can also be expressed either by a menos que or more formally by a no ser que. Both mean 'unless', and are always followed by the appropriate tense of the subjunctive:

saldremos mañana a menos que llueva/a no ser que llueva
we'll go out tomorrow unless it rains

6 Conditions introduced by conditional conjunctions

Conditional clauses introduced by conditional conjunctions always have their verb in the subjunctive. The most common of these conjunctions are:

en caso de que	if
a condición de que	on condition that, provided that
con tal que	so long as
siempre que	so long as

en caso de que venga, se lo diré
if he comes, I'll tell him

puedes salir con tal que prometas volver antes de medianoche
you can go out so long as you promise to be home by midnight

los compraremos a condición de que sean baratos
we'll buy them provided they're cheap

7 Points to note

Not all conditions are introduced in English by 'if'. Other forms are sometimes used. This choice is not available in Spanish. If you are translating, you must use si (or the de + infinitive construction) no matter what the form of the English condition:

had I known, I would have told you
si lo hubiera sabido/de haberlo sabido, te lo habría dicho

were this the case, I would agree with you
si fuera así/de ser así, estaría de acuerdo contigo

If si means 'whenever', it introduces a clause of time and only the indicative is used, not the subjunctive:

si tenía mucho que hacer, nunca salía antes de las nueve
if I had a lot to do, I never went out before nine

If si means 'whether' and introduces an indirect question, the subjunctive is not used either:

me preguntó si lo haría
he asked me if I would do it
(= whether I would)

no sé si vendrá
I don't know if he'll come
(= at all)

 ## C CONTRADICTING A PREVIOUS STATEMENT

1 pero and sino

The idea of 'but' is expressed by two words in Spanish, pero and sino. Sino is used to introduce a statement which contradicts a previous one. Pero *cannot* be used in such situations. Compare:

el coche es grande pero no cuesta mucho
the car is big but it doesn't cost a lot

el coche no es verde, sino rojo
the car isn't green, but red

mi padre no es médico, sino profesor
my father isn't a doctor, but a teacher

If the contradiction is contained in a clause, sino que is used:

no se come, sino que se bebe
you don't eat it, you drink it

If the intention is not to contradict, but to emphasise a following affirmation, pero sí is used:

no conozco a España, pero sí conozco a Portugal
I don't know Spain, but I do know Portugal

no es moderno, pero sí interesante
it isn't modern, but it is interesting

2 no es que, no porque

Both of these expressions are followed by a verb in the subjunctive:

no es que no tenga confianza en ti
it's not that I don't trust you

lo hace no porque quiera hacerlo, sino porque no tiene más remedio
he does it not because he wants to, but because he has no choice

D DISCOUNTING A DIFFICULTY

1 'despite'

The simplest way of discounting a difficulty is to use the compound preposition a pesar de followed by the noun. In written Spanish, pese a is sometimes used instead of a pesar de:

decidió continuar a pesar de las dificultades
he decided to continue in spite of the difficulties

2 'although'

The idea of 'although' can be expressed either by aunque or a pesar de que. In written Spanish si bien is a fairly frequent alternative to aunque, though it is little used in the spoken language.

Aunque may be followed by either the indicative or the subjunctive, depending on the speaker's perception of the difficulty. The indicative suggests a real difficulty, whereas the subjunctive implies a potential difficulty:

no se ha puesto el abrigo aunque hace mucho frío
he hasn't put on his coat even though it's very cold

continuaremos aunque haya problemas
we'll continue even though there may be problems

A pesar de que is used mostly with reference to present and past time and is therefore usually followed by the indicative:

lo hizo a pesar de que nadie estaba de acuerdo con él
he did it even though nobody agreed with him

Si bien is always followed by the indicative:

se cambiará la ley, si bien hay mucha oposición
the law will be changed although there is a lot of opposition

In written Spanish, con + infinitive is sometimes used to express the idea of 'although', though this is not a common usage:

con ser pobres, viven bien
although they're poor, they live well

3 'however'/'no matter how' + adjective or adverb + verb

This idea is expressed as follows in Spanish: por + adjective or adverb + que + verb in the subjunctive:

las compraremos, por caras que sean
we'll buy them, however expensive they are (might be)

no dejaré de hacerlo, por difícil que parezca
I won't fail to do it, no matter how difficult it might seem

por bien que lo haga, no lo aceptaré
however well she does it, I won't accept it

4 'whatever', 'however', 'wherever' *etc* + verb

There are two ways of expressing this idea in Spanish:

a) Verb in the subjunctive + relative + verb in the subjunctive. The same verb is repeated in this construction:

lo compraremos, cueste lo que cueste
we'll buy it, whatever it costs

no quiero verle, sea quien sea
I don't want to see him, whoever he is (might be)

le encontraremos, esté donde esté
we'll find him, wherever he is (might be)

b) Indefinite pronoun or adjective + que + verb in the subjunctive. The indefinite pronouns and adjectives are formed by adding -quiera to the end of the corresponding relative (there is no equivalent form for lo que):

no quiero verle, quienquiera que sea
I don't want to see him, whoever he is (might be)

le encontraremos, dondequiera que esté
we'll find him, wherever he is (might be)

If the pronoun or adjective is to be made plural, it is the part
before the -quiera which becomes plural while -quiera itself
remains unchanged:

no quiero verlos, quienesquiera que sean
I don't want to see them, whoever they are

E EMOTION/FEAR/HOPE/REGRET

1 Emotion

a) One subject

An expression of emotion where there is only one subject is
followed by the verb in the infinitive:

estamos muy contentos de veros
we are very pleased to see you

We are pleased, and we see you – there is only one subject.

espero poder hablar con él mañana
I hope to be able to speak to him tomorrow

b) More than one subject

However, if more than one subject is involved, the expression of
emotion is followed by a verb in the subjunctive. The range of
emotions goes from approval to disapproval, pleasure to anger
and the like:

me alegra que pienses así
I'm glad you feel that way

le molestó que no estuviéramos de acuerdo con él
it annoyed him that we did not agree with him

The expression of emotion may be implicit in an impersonal
construction:

es triste/lógico/natural/una pena que sea así
it's sad/logical/natural/a shame that it should be like this

All of these expressions imply an emotional reaction (however implicit) on the speaker's part rather than a straightforward statement of fact.

Note that the verb is in the subjunctive only if it belongs to a clause introduced by que which is *directly* dependent on the expression of emotion. If the clause is introduced by porque or if it is dependent on some other verb, the subjunctive is not used:

estaba triste porque todos le habían abandonado
he was sad because everyone had left him

se puso furioso al ver que nadie le escuchaba
he became furious when he saw that no-one was listening to him

In this case the clause is dependent on the verb ver, not on the expression of emotion.

2 Fear

a) 'to fear something', 'to be afraid of something'

The simplest way to express fear is to use a phrase such as tener miedo a, or less commonly the verb temer. Note that the preposition used with tener miedo can be either a or de (as opposed to only 'of' in 'to be afraid of' in English):

tengo miedo a los perros
I'm afraid of dogs

In colloquial Spanish, the phrase dar miedo may also be used. However, the object of the English verb becomes the subject of the Spanish verb, and the subject of the English verb becomes the indirect object of the Spanish verb (as with gustar, page 116):

me dan miedo las arañas
I'm afraid of spiders

b) 'to fear' + verb

The rules for one or more subjects mentioned earlier (*see* section E.1) also apply here:

me da miedo salir por la noche
I am afraid of going out at night

temo que surjan problemas imprevistos
I'm afraid that unforeseen problems might crop up

Note that the expression 'I'm afraid' is often used in English to introduce statements of fact or possibility where there is no real suggestion of any fear. Temer may also be used in this way in Spanish (it is frequently used reflexively in this context).
In this case temerse may be followed by either the indicative or the subjunctive. The indicative is used for a statement of fact. The subjunctive suggests the possibility that something may have happened:

me temo que lo ha/haya perdido
I'm afraid he's lost it/he may have lost it

c) Other expressions

Other expressions indicating genuine fear are also followed by the subjunctive:

se escondió por miedo a que se burlasen de él
he hid for fear that they would laugh at him

3 Hope

a) 'to hope for something'

This is expressed simply by esperar. The idea of 'for' is included in the verb, so that no preposition is used:

esperábamos una respuesta más positiva
we were hoping for a more positive reply

b) 'to hope' + verb

'To hope' is again usually expressed in this context by the verb esperar. With this meaning esperar may take either the indicative or the subjunctive (esperar meaning 'to wait' is *always* followed by the subjunctive).
When followed by the indicative esperar expresses keenness.

When followed by the subjunctive it expresses genuine hope.
Compare the following:

espero que vendrá (indicative)
I hope he'll come

I'm counting on him coming. I'll be disappointed/annoyed if he doesn't come.

espero que tengas éxito (subjunctive)
I hope you succeed

This is genuine hope, and does not have the connotations of 'counting on' mentioned above.

c) Impersonal expressions

Impersonal expressions of hope are followed by the subjunctive:

hay pocas esperanzas de que venga
there's little hope that he'll come

mi ilusión es que un día se resuelva el problema
my hope is that one day the problem will be solved

d) ojalá

In spoken Spanish ojalá is frequently used to introduce an expression of hope. Ojalá is invariable and never changes its form. It is always followed by the subjunctive:

ojalá no llueva mañana   **ojalá venga**
I hope it doesn't rain tomorrow   I hope he comes

4 Regret

a) Apologising for something

The simplest statements of apology are of course perdón, perdone (an imperative) and lo siento. They are different in that perdón and perdone are both requests for forgiveness, whereas lo siento is a direct expression of regret:

¡ay, perdona! no te vi
oh, sorry! I didn't see you

In this case the tú form of the imperative (perdona) is used.

lo siento, pero no será posible terminarlo hoy
sorry, but it won't be possible to finish it today

When the thing or action regretted is explicitly stated, the lo of lo siento is no longer used. The idea of 'for' is included in the verb and is not explicitly stated in Spanish:

sentimos la molestia
we are sorry/apologise for the inconvenience

In more formal Spanish, lamentar is often used in preference to sentir:

lamentamos la molestia que les hemos causado
we regret the inconvenience we have caused

b) 'to regret' + verb

If there is only one subject, the infinitive is used, otherwise a clause with the verb in the subjunctive is required:

sentimos tener que molestarle
we are sorry to have to bother you

sentimos mucho que no hayas podido hacerlo
we are very sorry that you were not able to do it

Again, the clause must be directly dependent on the verb expressing regret. If it is dependent on any other verb, the indicative will be used:

lamentamos informarles que ya no están disponibles
we are sorry to inform you that they are no longer available

The clause here is dependent on informar and not on lamentamos.

F INTENTIONS AND OBJECTIVES

1 Statements of intention

Simple statements of intention are expressed using the verb pensar or the phrase tener la intención de, both followed by the infinitive.

In spoken Spanish, the construction tener pensado + infinitive is also widely used.

pensamos ir en coche/tenemos la intención de ir en coche
we intend to go by car

tengo pensado salir esta noche
I intend to go out this evening

2 Statement of objectives

a) One subject

If only one person is involved, objectives are usually expressed by the preposition para followed by the infinitive. More formal alternatives are a fin de, con el fin de, con la intención de, con el objetivo de or con la finalidad de, all followed by the infinitive:

lo hice para ganar un poco de dinero
I did it to earn a little money

me dirijo a Vds. con el objetivo de pedir información
I am writing to you to ask for information

After verbs of motion, intention is usually expressed by the preposition a followed by the infinitive, though para is also possible:

vine aquí a hablar contigo
I came here to speak to you

Other verbs are followed by different prepositions (*see* pages 262-8):

luchaban por mejorar sus condiciones de vida
they were fighting to improve their living conditions

b) Two different subjects

If more than one subject is involved, para que followed by the subjunctive is necessary. A straightforward infinitive will be wrong in Spanish:

les ayudamos para que pudieran acabarlo pronto
we helped them so that they could get it done sooner

The more formal alternatives given earlier can also be used
followed by que and the subjunctive:

me voy, a fin de que puedan empezar inmediatamente
I'm going, so that they can start immediately

G OBLIGATION

1 General obligation

A number of constructions exist in Spanish to express obligation on
a very general level. The commonest of these are:

> **hay que** + infinitive
> **es preciso** + infinitive
> **es necesario** + infinitive

The degree of obligation can be heightened as follows:

> **es esencial** + infinitive
> **es imprescindible** + infinitive

These expressions are not addressed to any one person in particular.
They simply express a general obligation.

hay que tener cuidado
you (ie one) must be careful

¿hay que ser miembro para poder jugar aquí?
do I/you have to be a member to play here?

hay que verificarlo
it'll have to be checked

será necesario verificarlo con él
it will be necessary to check it with him

2 Personal obligation

More personal kinds of obligation (ie those affecting particular
people or groups of people) are expressed using the verb

deber + infinitive or the verb tener followed by que + infinitive:

> **debemos salir a las ocho en punto**
> we must leave at eight on the dot

> **tendrás que trabajar mucho**
> you'll have to work hard

> **tengo que terminarlo cuanto antes**
> I have to finish it as soon as possible

The sense of obligation can be heightened by using one of the phrases given in **section 1.** (with the exception of hay que) followed by que and a verb in the subjunctive:

> **es imprescindible que lo hagas ahora mismo**
> you absolutely must do it right now

Note that 'have to' in English does not always denote an obligation. For example, in the phrase 'I had to laugh', you were not, of course, obliged to laugh. This simply means that you could not stop yourself from laughing. This idea is expressed in Spanish as follows:

> **no pudimos por menos de reír**
> we had to laugh/could not help laughing

3 Moral obligation

Moral obligation is expressed in Spanish by the conditional (or less frequently the imperfect) of deber followed by the infinitive. This is usually expressed in English by 'should' or 'ought to':

> **deberíamos ir a verle**
> we should go and see him

This is not an obligation in the sense that we are being *forced* to go and see him, but we feel that it is our 'duty'.

Note

The use of 'should' in English to express moral obligation can *never* be translated into Spanish by the conditional. For example, **haría** can never express the idea of 'I ought to do'. Only **debería hacer** will convey this idea succesfully.

To put this idea into the past, use the perfect infinitive after the conditional of **deber**:

deberíamos haberlo hecho antes
we should have done it sooner

no deberías haber bebido tanto
you shouldn't have drunk so much

4 Obliging someone to do something

This idea is usually expressed by **obligar** or **forzar** + **a** + infinitive. Alternatively, **hacer** + infinitive can be used. The subject of the infinitive will be different from that of **obligar**:

me obligaron a salir
they forced me to leave

me hizo levantarme temprano
he made me get up early

When expressing the idea of 'being obliged to do something', **verse** is almost always used in preference to **ser**:

me vi obligado a devolverlo
I was obliged to give it back

 H PROBABILITY/IMPROBABILITY

The adverb **probablemente** (like all adverbs) has no effect on whether the verb is in the indicative or the subjunctive:

probablemente vendrá mañana
he'll probably come tomorrow

However, any impersonal expression of either probability or improbability is followed by a subordinate clause with its verb in the subjunctive:

es probable que salga por la tarde
I'll probably go out this evening (it's probable that I'll go out ...)

es improbable que vuelva
he's unlikely to come back (it's improbable that he'll come back)

me parece increíble que consiga hacerlo
I find it unlikely that he'll manage to do it

tenemos que aceptar la probabilidad de que esto ocurra
we must accept the likelihood that this will happen

 PERMISSION/PREVENTION/PROHIBITION

1 General permission and prohibition

The most general forms of permission and prohibition are expressed using the verb **poder**:

¿puedo pasar?   **no puedes pasar ahora**
may I come in?   you may not come in just now

¿se puede aparcar por aquí?
can you (ie one) park around here?

The prohibition corresponding to **se puede** is **se prohíbe, está prohibido** or simply **prohibido**. These are found mostly in official signs:

prohibido/se prohíbe pisar el césped
please do not walk on the grass

This can be emphasised as follows:

queda terminantemente prohibido cruzar la vía
crossing the line is strictly forbidden

2 Personal permission, prevention and prohibition

The commonest verbs of permitting, preventing and prohibiting belong to that group which may be followed by an infinitive with a different subject (*see* page 259). This usually avoids the need for a subordinate clause:

> **me dejaron entrar pero me impidieron verle**
> they let me go in but they prevented me from seeing him

> **nos prohibieron fumar**
> they did not allow us to smoke

Note the very common phrase:

> **¿me permite?**
> may I?

In many cases a straightforward imperative may be used:

> **no digas tacos**
> don't use bad words

J POSSIBILITY/IMPOSSIBILITY

1 In a personal sense

a) poder and related verbs

The simplest way of expressing possibility is to use the verb poder:

> **no podré venir mañana**
> I won't be able to come tomorrow

> **no habríamos podido hacerlo sin ti**
> we wouldn't have been able to do it without you

The verbs conseguir and lograr are used with the same meaning (of these conseguir is the more common):

> **no conseguimos llegar a tiempo**
> we didn't manage to arrive on time

> **logramos evitar un conflicto**
> we managed to avoid a conflict

A further alternative is to use the impersonal expression ser (im)posible. The person for whom the action is (im)possible becomes the indirect object:

no me será posible venir
I won't be able (it won't be possible for me) to come

nos fue imposible resolver el problema
we couldn't solve the problem

Resultar is sometimes used instead of ser:

me resultó imposible hacer lo que quería
I could not do what he wanted

b) saber

Note that 'to be able' in the sense of 'to know how to' rather than 'to be capable of' is expressed in Spanish by saber rather than poder:

¿sabes tocar la guitarra?
can you play the guitar?

sí, pero no sé tocar el piano
yes, but I can't play the piano

This is a skill rather than a physical ability.

c) Verbs of perception

'To be able' with verbs of perception (seeing, hearing and the like) is not usually expressed in Spanish unless you wish to suggest that there is some kind of obstacle involved:

¿me oyes?
can you hear me?

no podía verle por la niebla
I couldn't see him because of the fog

2 In a general sense

a) **quizá, quizás, tal vez**

Possibility in a more general sense (ie not 'being able to do something', but the possibility that something might happen or not) can be expressed by one of the adverbs quizás, quizá or tal vez. Quizás and quizá are more widely used.

These may be followed by either the indicative or the subjunctive, depending on your view of how likely it is that the thing will in fact happen. The indicative expresses a greater degree of confidence than the subjunctive:

quizás venga mañana, no sé (subjunctive)
he may come tomorrow, I don't know

tal vez tienes razón (indicative)
you may be right

b) Verbal forms

Poder can also be used to express a general possibility:

puede haber cambios importantes dentro de poco
there may be important changes soon

This idea can also be expressed by the impersonal expressions es posible que and puede que followed by the appropriate form of the subjunctive:

es posible que venga mañana
he may come tomorrow

puede que no sea verdad
it may not be true

In fact, any impersonal expression of possibility or chance is followed by the subjunctive:

existe la posibilidad de que surjan problemas
there is the possibility that problems will crop up

Note the following expression:

parece mentira que esto haya ocurrido
it seems impossible that this should have happened

REQUESTS AND COMMANDS

1 Direct requests

a) Informal requests

Spaniards are rather more direct in their requests than the average English speaker, who tends to introduce most requests with 'would you' and the like. A straightforward question is more likely in Spanish:

¿me pasas esa revista?
would you pass me that magazine?

¿me prestas diez euros?
would you lend me ten euros?

Alternatively, for a slightly less direct request, the appropriate form of **poder** + infinitive can be used ('could you' in English):

¿puedes abrir la ventana?
could you open the window?

¿podría decirme qué hora es?
could you tell me the time, please?

The expression **hacer el favor de** + infinitive is also used if a little more formality is required:

¿me hace el favor de cerrar la ventana?
would you be so kind as to close the window, please?

b) Formal requests

There are much more formal ways of introducing a request, particularly in written Spanish. The most common of these are the expressions **tenga(n) la bondad de** + infinitive and **le(s) ruego que** followed by the verb in the subjunctive:

tenga la bondad de cerrar la puerta
be so kind as to close the door

In the very formal Spanish of a business letter, the **que** is sometimes omitted after **le(s) ruego**. This usage should not be imitated in contexts other than commercial correspondence:

les rogamos nos manden dos cajas
please send us two boxes

c) Ultra-formal requests

In very formal Spanish, the old-fashioned form **sírvase** can still be found. This is in fact an imperative. If addressed to more than one person, **sírvanse** is used instead. This construction is restricted to commercial correspondence and official signs:

sírvanse mandarnos más información
please send us more information

2 Indirect requests

Since there are always at least two subjects involved in an indirect request, the verb is always followed by a subordinate clause with its verb in the subjunctive.

The most common verb used to introduce an indirect request is **pedir**. In more formal Spanish, **rogar** is again sometimes used in preference to **pedir**:

le pedí que se callara
I asked him to be quiet

nos rogaron que les ayudáramos
they asked us to help them

Note

Be careful not to confuse **pedir** and **preguntar**. **Preguntar** means 'to ask a *question*', and is used to introduce an indirect question. It does not involve the idea of a request: in that case you should use **pedir**. More intense requests can be expressed by verbs such as **suplicar**:

me suplicó que no revelara su secreto
he pleaded with me not to reveal his secret

---

3 Indirect commands

For direct commands (the imperative), see **pages 76, 231.**

There are always at least two subjects involved in an indirect command. Normally, this means a subordinate clause with the verb in the subjunctive:

me dijo que lo hiciera inmediatamente
he told me to do it immediately

insistimos en que nos lo devuelvan ahora mismo
we insist that you give it back to us right now

However, the verbs mandar and ordenar belong to that small group of verbs which can be used with a direct infinitive (*see* page 259):

me mandó salir del edificio
he ordered me to leave the building

L SUPPOSITION

1 Future tense

Apart from the usual verbs of supposition (for example suponer), the simplest way of expressing supposition in Spanish is to use the future tense for a supposition in the present, and a conditional for a supposition in the past. A similar construction exists in English, though it is less used than its Spanish equivalent:

supongo que vendrá
I imagine he'll come

¿qué hora es? – serán las once
what time is it – it must be about eleven (it'll be about eleven)

la casa estará por aquí
the house must be around here somewhere (will be around here somewhere)

serían las cinco más o menos cuando llegó
it must have been about five (it would be about five) when he arrived

2 deber de + infinitive

Supposition can also be expressed by the verb deber followed by de and the infinitive. Do not confuse this with deber followed by a direct infinitive, which expresses an obligation.

debes de estar cansado después de tanto trabajo
you must be tired after so much work

Note

False friend: the Spanish verb asumir does *not* mean 'to assume' in the sense of 'to suppose', but in the sense of 'to take on' as in 'to assume power'. 'Assume' in the sense of 'suppose' is translated either by suponer, or by one of the constructions explained above.

M THANKS

1 Simple expressions of thanks

a) gracias and related terms

The simplest expression of thanks is, of course, gracias. Since thanking someone always involves the idea of an exchange (you thank someone in exchange for what they have given you, or done for you), the preposition used with gracias is always por:

muchas gracias por el regalo
thanks a lot for the present

me dio las gracias por el regalo
he thanked me for the present

A verb used after gracias may be put into either the present infinitive or the perfect infinitive:

gracias por ayudarme/haberme ayudado
thanks for helping me

Likewise, any noun or adjective expressing thanks or gratitude is followed by **por**:

queremos expresar nuestro reconocimiento por todo
we want to express our gratitude for everything

b) agradecer

In more formal Spanish, **gracias** is almost always replaced by the appropriate form of the verb **agradecer**. **Agradecer** is an exception to what has been said above in that the idea of 'for' is contained within the verb:

> ## Note
>
> The verb **agradecer** is not followed by any kind of preposition in Spanish:
>
> **les agradecemos su cooperación en este asunto**
> we thank you for your cooperation in this matter
>
> **nos agradecieron nuestra ayuda**
> they thanked us for our help

2 Subordinate clauses

The verb in a subordinate clause following an expression of gratitude goes into the subjunctive. The commonest occurrences of such expressions are the following:

> **agradeceremos mucho que nos ayuden**
> **agradeceríamos mucho que nos ayudasen**

Both of these are Spanish equivalents of 'we would be grateful if you could help us'. Either may be used on any occasion, despite the difference in tenses. Note the idea of 'could' is not expressed in Spanish.

Unlike English, Spanish does not consider this kind of expression to be a condition, so no **si** clause is used.

In the very formal Spanish of business correspondence, the que may be omitted from this expression:

> **agradeceremos nos manden diez cajas**
> we would be grateful if you could send us ten boxes

This usage is not found in other contexts.

WISHES/DESIRES/PREFERENCES

1 One subject

If only one subject is involved, a straightforward infinitive is used:

> **quiero hablar contigo**
> I want to speak to you

> **preferiría salir ahora**
> I would prefer to leave now

> **valdría más empezar enseguida**
> it would be better to start right away

The expression of a wish can always be 'softened' in Spanish by using the imperfect subjunctive of querer:

> **quisiéramos comer ahora**
> we'd like to eat now

2 Two subjects

In this case the verb of wishing must be followed by a subordinate clause with its verb in the subjunctive:

> **quiero que lo hagan ellos mismos**
> I want them to do it themselves

> **me gustaría que Vds. empezaran enseguida**
> I would like you to start right away

> **hubiera preferido que escogieras otra cosa**
> I would have preferred you to choose something else

10 NUMBERS AND NUMBER-RELATED FUNCTIONS

A NUMBERS

1 The cardinal numbers

For the forms of the cardinal numbers, see **page 272**.

Note that, though most numbers are invariable (ie they never change their form), there are feminine forms of uno and of all the hundreds between 200 and 900 inclusive. It is a very common error not to make the hundreds agree:

me costó quinientas libras
it cost me five hundred pounds

Uno also agrees in compound numbers:

veintiuna ovejas
twenty-one sheep

Note that 'one' is not expressed in phrases such as the following:

¿qué coche prefieres? – el rojo
which car do you prefer? – the red one

No article is used with cien or mil, or with the adjective medio:

cien mil soldados
one hundred thousand soldiers

esperamos media hora
we waited for half an hour

Note that both millón and billón are nouns and *must* be followed by de:

el gobierno invertirá diez millones de euros
the government will invest ten million euros

Un billón in Spanish still means one million million (in most other countries the term 'billion' has come to mean one thousand million). In the Spanish press, the word billón is frequently written in italics to highlight this difference.

2 The ordinal numbers

For the formation of the ordinal numbers, see page 274.

These are seldom used beyond décimo, being usually replaced by the cardinal numbers:

vivo en el tercer piso
I live on the third floor

but:

en el siglo veinte   **en la página treinta y dos**
in the twentieth century   on page thirty-two

3 Approximate numbers

An approximate number can be made from any multiple of ten by dropping the final vowel and adding the ending -ena, though such numbers are in fact very rare beyond forty:

una veintena de muchachos
about twenty boys

Some other numbers also formed with this ending have become words in their own right:

una docena   **una quincena**
a dozen   a fortnight

The approximate numbers corresponding to **ciento** and **mil** are **centenar** and **millar**, though **cientos** and **miles** may also be used:

> **vinieron millares de hinchas**
> thousands of fans turned up

Approximate numbers can also be expressed by a variety of terms such as **en torno a**, **alrededor de**, **aproximadamente**, **más o menos**, or the plural article **unos** (**a eso de** is limited to expressions of time):

> **había aproximadamente cincuenta personas en la sala**
> there were about fifty people in the room

> **llegaron unos diez hombres**
> about ten men arrived

> **cuesta unas dos mil euros**
> it costs about two thousand euros

Note also the following:

> **se lo dije hasta veinte veces**
> I told him as many as twenty times

> **por lo menos doscientos**
> at least two hundred

> **cuarenta y tantos**
> forty odd

> **unos pocos/unos cuantos**
> a few

4 Fractions and decimals

a) Fractions

Note that, when used with another number, the phrase **y medio** comes after the *noun* and not after the number as in English:

> **dos horas y media**
> two and a half hours

This also applies in the case of the nouns millón and billón:

seis millones y medio de turistas británicos
six and a half million British tourists

b) Decimals

Spaniards use a comma to indicate a decimal fraction, and not a point as in English:

dos coma siete por ciento (2,7 por 100)
two point seven per cent

In colloquial Spanish, the word coma is often replaced by con:

cinco con cuatro millones (5,4 millones)
five point four million

B TIME

1 Translating the word 'time'

There are several words in Spanish for 'time'. They all have different meanings and must not be confused:

la hora	time on the clock
la época	a period of time of unspecified duration but not measured by the clock
el tiempo	time in general
la vez	an occasion

quizás podríamos vernos a una hora conveniente
perhaps we could meet at a convenient time

siempre hay muchos turistas en esta época del año
there are always lots of tourists at this time of year

pasó mucho tiempo en España
he spent a long time in Spain

ya te lo he dicho por lo menos diez veces
I've already told you at least ten times

Note also the following:

> **de una vez por todas**
> once and for all
>
> **a la tercera va la vencida** (Spanish proverb)
> third time lucky

2 Time on the clock

Time on the clock is expressed as follows:

¿qué hora es? what time is it?	**es la una** it's one o'clock
son las tres it's three o'clock	**son las diez** it's ten o'clock

The feminine definite articles are used because the word understood but not expressed is hora or horas. Time after the hour is expressed as follows:

son las tres y cinco it's five past three	**son las siete y cuarto** it's a quarter past seven
son las ocho y veinticinco it's twenty-five past eight	**son las once y media** it's half past eleven

Time to the hour:

es la una menos diez it's ten to one	**son las cuatro menos cuarto** it's a quarter to four

'At' is expressed by a:

a mediodía, a medianoche at midday, at midnight	**a las seis y diez** at ten past six

Note also:

a las diez en punto at ten o'clock on the dot	**a eso de las ocho** at around eight o'clock
a las tres y pico just after three	**¿qué hora tienes?** what time do you make it?
tengo las ocho I make it eight o'clock	**daban las diez** it was striking ten o'clock

For the purposes of specifying time, the Spanish day is divided into more sections than its English equivalent:

la madrugada	from midnight till dawn
la mañana	from dawn till noon
el mediodía	from noon till early afternoon
la tarde	from early afternoon till dark
la noche	from nightfall till midnight

Madrugada can be replaced by mañana. The use of madrugada emphasises the fact that the speaker considers the time in question to be very early (or very late) from his point of view:

me levanté/me acosté a las dos de la madrugada
I got up/went to bed at two in the morning

a las tres de la madrugada
at three in the morning

a las diez de la mañana
at ten in the morning

a la una del mediodía
at one in the afternoon

a las cinco de la tarde
at five in the evening

a las diez de la noche
at ten in the evening

The twenty-four hour clock is also used in timetables and official announcements, though it is not used conversationally:

a las quince treinta y cinco
at fifteen thirty-five

If no specific time of day is mentioned, broad time of day is expressed using the preposition por:

salieron por la mañana
they went out in the morning

volveremos por la tarde
we'll come back in the afternoon

Note also the following:

anoche	last night
ayer	yesterday
antes de ayer/anteayer	the day before yesterday
mañana	tomorrow
pasado mañana	the day after tomorrow
ayer por la mañana	yesterday morning
mañana por la noche	tomorrow evening
dos veces por hora	twice an hour
ochenta kilómetros por hora	eighty kilometres an hour

3 Days of the week

For a list of days, months and seasons, see page 276.

Days of the week are written with a small letter. 'On' is expressed simply by the definite article. No preposition is used:

fuimos al cinema el sábado
we went to the cinema on Saturday

vamos a la playa los domingos
we go to the beach on Sundays

el lunes/los lunes por la mañana
on Monday morning/mornings

Note also:

el miércoles pasado	last Wednesday
el sábado que viene	next Saturday
dos veces al día	twice a day
cinco veces a la semana	five times a week
mil euros por semana	a thousand euros per week

4 The date

The months are written with a small letter. 'The first' may be expressed as el primero or el uno. All other dates are expressed only by the appropriate cardinal number (ie three, four *etc* not third, fourth *etc*).

'On' is expressed simply by the definite article, or by placing el día in front of the number. The only exception is in the heading to a letter, where no article is used:

> ¿a cuántos estamos hoy?/¿a qué día del mes estamos?/¿qué día es hoy?
> what date is it today?

> hoy estamos a dos
> today is the second

> llegaremos el 12 de marzo
> we will arrive on 12 March

> salieron el día 9
> they left on the 9th

In a full date, both the month and the year are introduced by de:

> el quince de octubre de mil novecientos ochenta y ocho
> the fifteenth of October nineteen eighty-eight

Note also:

el siglo veinte	the twentieth century
el siglo dieciocho	the eighteenth century
en los años treinta	in the thirties
la España de los años ochenta	the Spain of the eighties
a principios/primeros de enero	at the beginning of January
a mediados de marzo	in the middle of March
a finales/fines de octubre	at the end of October
dos veces al mes	twice a month
cuatro veces al año	four times a year
en lo que va de año	this year so far
a lo largo del año	throughout the year

5 The seasons

The names of the seasons are preceded by a definite article unless used with en:

la primavera es muy agradable en España
spring is very pleasant in Spain

iremos a España en otoño
we're going to Spain in the autumn

6 Age

Age is expressed as follows:

¿cuántos años tienes?   **tengo diecisiete años**
how old are you?   I'm seventeen

¿qué edad tiene tu hermano?
what age is your brother?

Note also the following:

ronda los cuarenta   **hoy cumplo veinte años**
he's getting on for forty   I'm twenty today

la juventud   **la tercera edad**
youth, young people   senior citizens, OAPs

7 Some useful expressions of time

hoy en día, hoy día	nowadays
hoy por hoy	nowadays
en la actualidad	nowadays
a corto/medio/largo plazo	in the short/medium/long term
hace diez años	ten years ago
diez años antes	ten years earlier
a partir de ahora	from now on
de aquí/hoy en adelante	from now on
en el futuro	in future

en el porvenir	in future
en lo sucesivo *(formal)*	in future
en lo venidero *(formal)*	in future
en los años venideros	in the years to come
al día siguiente	the following day
la próxima semana	next week
la semana que viene	next week
la semana pasada	last week
la semana siguiente	the next week
la semana anterior	the previous week

C PRICES/MEASUREMENTS/PERCENTAGES

1 Prices

Rate in prices is expressed by the definite article:

este vino cuesta tres euros el litro
this wine costs three euros a litre

lo vendían a seis euros el kilo
they were selling it at six euros a kilo

Note also:

¿cuánto cuestan/valen las manzanas?/¿a cómo se venden las manzanas?
how much are the apples?

2 Measurements

Measurements may be expressed using either the adjective or the noun relating to the measurement in question (length, height, breadth *etc*):

¿cuál es la altura del muro?
how high is the wall?

el muro tiene dos metros de alto/altura
the wall is two metres high

la calle tiene cien metros de largo/longitud
the street is one hundred metres long

Note that in the following construction the adjective agrees:

una calle de cien metros de larga
a street one hundred metres long

Note also:

¿cuánto pesas?
what do you weigh?

¿cuánto mides?
how tall are you?

mide casi dos metros
he's almost two metres tall

tiene una superficie de cien metros cuadrados
it has a surface area of one hundred square metres

tiene una capacidad de dos metros cúbicos
it has a capacity of two cubic metres

Distance is always indicated by the preposition **a**:

¿a qué distancia está la playa? – a unos cinco kilómetros
how far away is the beach? – about five kilometres

3 Percentages

Percentages in Spanish are invariably preceded by either a definite or an indefinite article. There is no difference in meaning:

la inflación ha aumentado en un diez por ciento
inflation has gone up ten per cent

el treinta por ciento de las personas entrevistadas no contestó
thirty per cent of those interviewed did not give an answer

Percentages are usually written in Spanish as 5 por 100 and the like. 100 por 100 is almost invariably pronounced cien por cien.

The amount by which a percentage increases or decreases is indicated in Spanish by the preposition en. The commonest verbs used in this connection are:

Increase:

aumentar, incrementar, crecer, subir

Decrease:

caer, bajar, reducir(se)

hemos reducido nuestros precios en un 15 por 100
we have reduced our prices by 15 per cent

If a percentage is not involved, normally no preposition is used:

las acciones han bajado un par de euros
shares have come down by a few euros

11 SENTENCE STRUCTURE

Sentence structure is not the same as word order. Sentence structure concerns the place occupied by the different *component parts* of the sentence, rather than *individual words*. Any of these component parts can consist of a number of words. For example, in a sentence such as the following:

el padre del amigo de mi hermano trabaja en Santander
my brother's friend's father works in Santander

the words **el padre del amigo de mi hermano** all go together to form the subject of the verb **trabaja**. The verb itself occupies the second *place* in the sentence, although it is the eighth *word*.

The most important elements of any sentence are the verb, the subject of the verb (ie who or what is carrying out the action of the verb), and the object or complement. A transitive verb takes an object, an intransitive verb is followed by a complement. There are other elements – adverbs, prepositional phrases *etc* – but these are less important and are not dealt with here.

1 English sentence structure

Sentence structure is very predictable in English. Most English sentences follow the order subject – verb – object/complement, eg:

Subject	*Verb*	*Object/Complement*
the boys	watch	the television (object)
Spanish	is	easy (complement)

The only consistent exception to this order in English is found in questions, where the order verb – subject – object/complement is more common:

Verb	*Subject*	*Object/Complement*
is	Spanish	easy?

2 Spanish sentence structure

Sentence structure is *very* much more flexible in Spanish than it is in English. This is not to suggest that the order subject – verb – object/complement is in any sense uncommon in Spanish. On the contrary, it is probably the commonest pattern in spoken Spanish, and is also commonly used in questions. Nonetheless, it is nowhere near as dominant in Spanish as it is in English, and a Spanish speaker will happily place the verb before the subject, and on occasions will even place the object before the verb.

There are few rules governing sentence structure in Spanish, but in general it could be said that:

– the closer any element of the sentence is to the beginning of the sentence, the more emphasis it receives, the first position in the sentence being obviously the most emphatic;

– it is unusual for the verb not to occupy the first or second *position* in the sentence (see the difference between position and word order given above).

The choice made by a Spanish speaker may be based on reasons of emphasis, but more often it will have to do with the rhythm of the sentence. Rhythms are not something which can be taught. A feeling for such rhythms can be obtained only through exposure to large amounts of genuine spoken Spanish.

3 Examples of different sentence structures

a) subject – verb

mi hermano está estudiando inglés
my brother is studying English

¿el coche está en el garaje?
is the car in the garage?

b) verb – subject

> **llegaron dos tíos y se pusieron a trabajar**
> two fellows came along and started to work

> **me lo dijo una vez mi padre**
> my father told me so once

c) object – verb – subject

> **el cuadro lo pintó un amigo mío**
> one of my friends painted the picture

> **la moto la compramos Juan y yo**
> Juan and I bought the motorbike

Note that when the object is placed before the verb, the corresponding object pronoun *must* also be placed before the verb.

d) use of first position for emphasis

> **a mí no me gusta nada**   **a ella no la puede ver**
> I don't like it at all   he can't stand her

> **tal decisión no la apoyaremos nunca**
> we shall never support such a decision

4 Punctuation

Punctuation in Spanish is by and large identical to English. Remember, however, that the upside-down question marks and exclamation marks are written at the beginning of the question and of the exclamation respectively. This is not necessarily at the beginning of the sentence:

> **¿qué quieres tomar?**   **y éste, ¿cuánto cuesta?**
> what will you have?   and how much does this one cost?

> **estuviste anoche en la discoteca, ¿verdad?**
> you were at the club last night, weren't you?

> **el público gritó '¡olé!'**
> the crowd shouted 'olé!'

PART II
FORMS

1 ACCENTUATION

Written accents in Spanish relate primarily to *spoken* stress. If you
know how a word is pronounced, you can tell by applying a few
simple rules if it requires a written accent, and, if so, where the
accent should be written.

1 Syllables

In order to know when and where to write an accent, it is
important to understand what is meant by a 'syllable'. A syllable
is a group of letters within a word at least one of which must be
a vowel. If there is no vowel, there is no syllable. In many cases,
the number of syllables in a word is the same as the number of
vowels:

- ca-sa (two syllables)
- con-cen-tra-da (four syllables)

If there are one or more consonants between each vowel, as
in the examples just given, the division into syllables is quite
straightforward. However, the situation is slightly more complex
if two or more vowels are written together.

Vowels in Spanish are divided into strong and weak vowels:

- the strong vowels are: A, E and O
- the weak vowels are: I and U

The rules regarding whether or not two or more vowels written
together form one or more syllables are as follows:

a) When two strong vowels appear together they belong to two
distinct syllables:

pa-se-ar (three syllables)
pe-or (two syllables)

b) When a strong and weak vowel appear together and there is no written accent on any of the weak vowels, they form only one syllable, and the strong vowel takes the stress:

fu*er*-te (two syllables)

vi*e*-jo (two syllables)

an-ci*a*-no (three syllables)

If one of the weak vowels is accentuated, it forms a separate syllable:

ha-cí-a (three syllables)

pú-a (two syllables)

c) When two or more weak vowels appear together they form only one syllable and the stress falls on the second vowel:

vi*u*-da (two syllables)

fu*í* (one syllable)

These rules apply to *pronunciation* only, and are unaffected by the way a word is written. For example, the o and i of prohibir belong to the same syllable, despite the fact that there is a written (but completely unpronounced) h between them. The e and u of rehusar belong to the same syllable for the same reason.

2 Spoken stress

All words in Spanish have one main stressed vowel, and it is the position of this stressed vowel in the word which determines whether or not there is a written accent. The rules for spoken stress are as follows:

a) The stress falls naturally on the second last syllable of the word when:

- the word ends in a vowel:
  ll*a*-mo, re-b*a*-ño, v*e*-o, v*a*-rio, re-ci-bi*e*-ra

- the word ends in -n or -s:
  c*a*n-tan, l*i*-bros, j*o*-ven

b) The stress falls naturally on the last syllable when the word ends in a consonant other than -n and -s:

can-t*a*r, ciu-d*a*d, no-mi-n*a*l

3 Primary use of the written accent

The written accent is mainly used in Spanish to show deviations from the rules for natural spoken stress given above. The pronunciation of the vowel on which the accent is written is not otherwise affected.

If the stress falls where the rules say it should fall, there is no written accent. If it does not, a written accent is placed over the vowel actually carrying the stress. This accounts for the overwhelming majority of cases of written accents in Spanish.

The general rules are, therefore:

– If a word ending in a vowel, -n or -s is *not* stressed on the second last syllable, a written accent is placed on the vowel which is in fact stressed: men*ú*, regi*ó*n, ingl*é*s

– If a word ending in a consonant other than -n or -s is not stressed on the last syllable, a written accent is placed on the vowel which is in fact stressed: c*é*sped, f*á*cil

More specifically, it can be seen that:

– Any word stressed on the third last syllable carries an accent on the stressed vowel irrespective of its ending: m*ú*sica, r*é*gimen

– Any word ending in a stressed vowel carries an accent on that vowel: caf*é*, rub*í*

– In any combination of a weak vowel and a strong vowel where it is the weak vowel which carries the stress, this weak vowel will have a written accent: quer*í*a, vac*í*o

Further examples:

Stress in 'natural' position (no accent)		*Stress out of position (written accent)*	
varias	several	**varías**	you vary
continuo	continuous	**continúo**	I continue
amar	to love	**ámbar**	amber
fabrica	he manufactures	**fábrica**	factory

Remember again that what counts is pronunciation and not spelling. The written accent on prohíbo or rehúso is explained by the fact that the weak vowel in the spoken syllables oi and eu is stressed.

Note also that written accents may have to be omitted from or added to plural forms:

> región – regiones
> joven – jóvenes

4 Secondary uses of the written accent

Other uses of the written accent are:

– to differentiate between two words which have the same spelling:

el (the)	**él** (he)
tu (your)	**tú** (you)
mi (my)	**mí** (me)
si (if)	**sí** (yes)
de (of)	**dé** (give)

– to identify the interrogative and exclamatory forms of certain pronouns and adverbs:

donde – ¿dónde?	**quien – ¿quién?**
where – where?	who – who?

– to differentiate the pronoun forms from the adjectival forms of the demonstratives (the pronouns are written with an accent):

este – éste	**aquella – aquélla**
this – this one	that – that one

Since the neuter pronouns cannot be confused with any other forms, no accent is required:

esto	**eso**	**aquello**
this (one)	that (one)	that (one)

5 The dieresis

A dieresis is only ever written over the letter u in Spanish, in which case it appears as ü. The dieresis occurs only in the combinations güe and güi, and indicates that the ü is to be pronounced as a separate vowel. If no dieresis is present, the u is not pronounced:

la cigüeña	**la vergüenza**
the stork	shame
la lingüística	**el piragüismo**
linguistics	canoeing

Compare these with words such as **la guerra, la guirnalda** and the like, where the u is not pronounced.

Note that a dieresis must sometimes be added or indeed omitted in certain forms of certain verbs, to ensure that the pronunciation of the verb is correctly reflected in the spelling, eg:

averiguo (*indicative*: I find out)
averigüe (*subjunctive*)

avergonzarse (*infinitive*: to be ashamed)
me avergüenzo (*first person singular*)

arguyo (*first person singular*)
argüir (*infinitive*: to argue)

2 GENDER

In Spanish all nouns are either *masculine* or *feminine*. There is no equivalent of the English neuter gender for nouns.

All words used with any noun (adjectives, articles *etc*) take the same gender as the noun.

1 Gender by ending

The gender of a noun can often be deduced from its ending:

a) Most nouns ending in -o are masculine:

el libro	**el dinero**	**el piano**
the book	the money	the piano

There are a few common exceptions:

la radio	**la mano**
the radio	the hand

b) Most nouns ending in -a are feminine:

la aduana	**la casa**	**la mañana**
the Customs	the house	the morning

Some common exceptions to this:

el día	**el mapa**	**el idioma**	**el clima**
the day	the map	the language	the climate

Also, most nouns ending in -ema and a few ending in -ama are masculine:

el problema	**el sistema**	**el lema**
the problem	the system	the slogan

el programa	**el drama**	**el telegrama**
the program	the drama	the telegram

c) Almost all nouns ending in -d are feminine:

la ciudad	**la vid**
the city	the vine
la pared	**la dificultad**
the wall	the difficulty
la juventud	
youth	

d) Almost all nouns ending in -ión are feminine:

la nación	**la región**
the nation	the region

There are a few common exceptions:

el camión	**el avión**
the lorry	the plane

2 Gender by meaning

a) People and animals

When referring to people and animals, often, though not always, the meaning of the noun decides its gender, eg:

el hombre	**la mujer**
the man	the woman
la vaca	
the cow	

However, there are some exceptions to the above, for example la víctima is the Spanish for a victim of either sex.

b) Some nouns are going through a period of transition:

El juez is the Spanish for 'judge' in general, but, as more women judges are appointed in Spain, you will now hear and read both la juez and la jueza.

Such alternative forms can coexist for some time. For example, Mrs. Thatcher was referred to in the Spanish press as la Primer Ministro and la Primera Ministra.

c) Words with both genders

There are many words ending in -ista, which can be either masculine or feminine, according to the gender of the person referred to:

el socialista, la socialista
the socialist

el periodista, la periodista
the journalist

Note

There is no separate 'masculine' form of these nouns – all the masculine forms end in -ista, like the feminines.

d) Nouns with corresponding forms for both genders

Some nouns may have both genders, depending on the gender of the person described:

el camarero	**la camarera**
the waiter	the waitress
el niño	**la niña**
the boy	the girl

Sometimes, a more substantial change of spelling is required:

el director	**la directriz**
the manager	the manageress
el actor	**la actriz**
the actor	the actress

e) Nouns with different meanings for different genders

Some nouns may appear with either gender, but their meanings change:

el policía the policeman	**la policía** the police force
el guía the guide (*person*)	**la guía** the guidebook
el capital capital (*money*)	**la capital** the capital city
el cura the parish priest	**la cura** the cure
el pendiente the earring	**la pendiente** the slope
el moral the mulberry bush	**la moral** ethics

3 THE NOUN – PLURAL OF NOUNS

1 Formation

The plural of Spanish nouns is formed as follows:

a) Adding -s to nouns ending in an unstressed vowel:

los libros	**las reglas**
the books	the rulers

b) Most nouns ending in a stressed vowel add -es:

el rubí	**los rubíes**
the ruby	the rubies

but some common nouns only add -s:

los cafés	**las mamás**	**los papás**
the cafes	the mums	the dads

c) Adding -es to nouns ending in a consonant other than -s:

los señores	**las tempestades**
the men	the storms

d) Nouns already ending in -s

If the last syllable is stressed, add -es:

el inglés	**los ingleses**
the Englishman	(the) Englishmen

However, if the last syllable is not stressed, the word does not change:

el lunes	**los lunes**
Monday	Mondays

e) Some nouns require a spelling change in the plural

Where nouns end in -z, this changes to -ces:

la actriz	**las actrices**
the actress	the actresses

f) Changes in written accent

Most singular nouns having a written accent on the last syllable lose this accent in the plural as it is no longer necessary:

la nación	**las naciones**
the nation	the nations

The few nouns ending in -n and which are stressed on the second last syllable in the singular need a written accent in the plural:

el joven	**los jóvenes**
the young man	the young men
el crimen	**los crímenes**
the crime	the crimes

g) There are two plurals in Spanish which actually change their accentuation from the singular to the plural form:

el carácter	**los caracteres**
the character	the characters
el régimen	**los regímenes**
the regime	the regimes

h) In the case of acronyms, plural forms are indicated by doubling the initials:

EE.UU.	**Estados Unidos** (USA)
CC.OO.	**Comisiones Obreras** (Trade Union)
FF.AA.	**Fuerzas Armadas** (Armed Forces)

i) Most English words used in Spanish keep the form of the English plural:

el camping	→	**los campings**
el poster	→	**los posters**
el comic	→	**los comics**

However, some English words which have been used in Spanish for a long time have also adopted a Spanish plural:

el club	→	**los clubes**
el bar	→	**los bares**
el superman	→	**los supermanes**

2 Special use of the masculine plural

The masculine plural form is frequently used to indicate both genders:

mis padres
my parents

los Reyes
the King and Queen

mis tíos
my aunt and uncle

4 THE ARTICLES

1 The definite article

a) The standard form

The definite article ('the') has both a masculine and a feminine form, each of which can also be put into the plural:

	MASCULINE	FEMININE
singular	el	la
plural	los	las

el señor	**los señores**
the man	the men

la chica	**las chicas**
the girl	the girls

b) A special feminine form

Note that the form of the feminine definite article used immediately before nouns which begin with a stressed a- or ha- is el and not la:

el agua
the water

el hambre
hunger

This change does not affect the *gender* of the noun. Other words accompanying the noun continue to take the feminine form:

el agua está fría
the water is cold

c) Contraction of the definite article

The masculine definite article joins together with the prepositions **a** and **de** to give the following forms:

a + el = al
de + el = del

fui al cine   **la casa del profesor**
I went to the cinema   the teacher's house

This does not happen if the **el** is part of a title in capital letters:

escribí a El Diario
I wrote to El Diario

However, feminines and plurals *never* contract.

d) Countries whose names are preceded by the definite article

The names of the following countries are preceded by the appropriate form of the definite article:

el Brasil	Brazil
el Ecuador	Ecuador
la India	India
el Japón	Japan
el Perú	Peru
el Uruguay	Uruguay

2 The indefinite article

a) The standard form

The indefinite article ('a') has both a masculine and a feminine form. Unlike English, both of these can also be put into the plural.

	MASCULINE	FEMININE
singular	un	una
plural	unos	unas

un hombre   **una cantidad**
a man   a quantity

b) A special feminine form

Note that the form of the feminine indefinite article used immediately before nouns which begin with a stressed a- or ha- is un:

un hacha	**un ala**
an axe	a wing

This change does not affect the *gender* of the noun. Other words accompanying the noun continue to take the feminine form:

construyeron un ala nueva
they built a new wing

c) The plural forms are used:

- with nouns which exist only in the plural or are normally used in the plural;
- to express the idea of 'some', 'a few'.

Otherwise, they are not required:

compré unos pantalones
I bought a pair of trousers

tengo un libro	**tengo unos libros**	**tengo libros**
I have a book	I have some books	I have books

5 THE DEMONSTRATIVES

1 The demonstrative adjectives

The demonstrative adjectives in Spanish are este (this) and ese and aquel (both meaning 'that'). Their forms are as follows:

	MASCULINE	FEMININE
singular	este	esta
plural	estos	estas
singular	ese	esa
plural	esos	esas
singular	aquel	aquella
plural	aquellos	aquellas

The demonstrative adjectives are placed *before* the noun:

este mes	**ese sillón**	**aquella bicicleta**
this month	that armchair	that bike

For usage, see pages 30-1.

2 The demonstrative pronouns

The demonstrative pronouns are identical to the demonstrative adjectives with the single exception that they carry a written accent on the stressed vowel:

este, éstos, ésta, éstas
ése, ésos, ésa, ésas
aquél, aquéllos, aquélla, aquéllas

There is also a neuter form which is *not* written with an accent (*see* page 32):

esto, eso, aquello

For usage, see pages 31-2.

6 THE POSSESSIVE ADJECTIVES AND PRONOUNS

1 The weak possessive adjectives

The weak possessive adjectives are placed before the noun. Their forms are as follows:

	MASC. SING	FEM. SING.	MASC. PLURAL	FEM. PLURAL
my	mi	mi	mis	mis
your	tu	tu	tus	tus
his/her/its/your	su	su	sus	sus
our	nuestro	nuestra	nuestros	nuestras
your	vuestro	vuestra	vuestros	vuestras
their/your	su	su	sus	sus

mi cuchillo my knife	**mis cuchillos** my knives	**mi cuchara** my spoon	**mis cucharas** my spoons
tu pañuelo your handkerchief	**tus pañuelos** your handkerchiefs	**tu chaqueta** your jacket	**tus chaquetas** your jackets
su saco his/her/your sack	**sus sacos** his/her/your sack	**su maleta** his/her/your suitcase	**sus maletas** his/her/your suitcases
nuestro piso our flat	**nuestros pisos** our flats	**nuestra casa** our house	**nuestras casas** our houses
vuestro coche your car	**vuestros coches** your cars	**vuestra casa** your house	**vuestras casas** your houses

| **su saco** | **sus sacos** | **su maleta** | **sus maletas** |
| your/their sack | your/their sack | your/their suitcase | your/their suitcases |

For a fuller treatment of su *and* sus, *see* page 38.

2 The strong possessive adjectives and pronouns

The strong possessive adjectives and the possessive pronouns are identical in form. They are as follows:

MASC. SING.	FEM. SING.	MASC. PLURAL	FEM. PLURAL
mío	mía	míos	mías
tuyo	tuya	tuyos	tuyas
suyo	suya	suyos	suyas
nuestro	nuestra	nuestros	nuestras
vuestro	vuestra	vuestros	vuestras
suyo	suya	suyos	suyas

For usage explanations, see pages 37-8.

7 AUGMENTATIVES AND DIMINUTIVES

1 The augmentatives

a) The following suffixes are added to nouns, adjectives, participles and adverbs as augmentatives (*see* pages 42–3):

masculine	-ón	-azo	-acho	-ote
feminine	-ona	-aza	-acha	-ota

b) Any vowel at the end of the original word is dropped.

un muchachazo
a big boy

un hombrote
a big man

2 The diminutives

a) The following suffixes are added to nouns, adjectives, participles and adverbs as diminutives (*see* pages 42–3):

-ito	*longer forms:*	-cito, -ecito
-illo	*longer forms:*	-cillo, -ecillo
-uelo	*longer forms:*	-zuelo, -ezuelo
-ín	*(no longer forms)*	
-ucho	*(no longer forms)*	

All of these endings can be made feminine by changing the -o to -a (-ín becomes -ina).

b) When the word ends in a vowel, this is dropped:

Ana	→	Anita
señora	→	señorita

c) Of the longer forms, -cito, -cillo and -zuelo are used with words of more than one syllable which end in -n or -r:

| salón | → | saloncito |
| calor | → | calorcito |

d) The forms -ecito, -ecillo and -ezuelo are used with words of one syllable:

| flor | → | florecita, florecilla |
| pez | → | pececito, pececillo |

Note that spelling changes (z to c) may be necessary.

They are also used with words of two syllables when the first syllable is -ie or -ue. The final vowel is dropped:

| pueblo | → | pueblecito |
| nieto | → | nietecito |

e) Written accents are dropped from the ending of the original word when a suffix is added:

| salón | → | saloncito |

A written accent is added to the weak vowel of the suffix when the original word ends in an accentuated vowel:

| mamá | → | mamaíta |

8 THE ADJECTIVE

1 Shortened form of adjectives

a) Certain adjectives drop the -o from the masculine singular immediately before the noun:

alguno	¿hay *algún* autobús por aquí? are there any buses around here?
ninguno	no veo *ningún* tren I don't see any trains
bueno	un *buen* vino a good wine
malo	el *mal* tiempo the bad weather
primero	el *primer* día del año the first day of the year
tercero	el *tercer* edificio the third building

Note that ninguno and alguno require a written accent when shortened in this way.

b) Grande is shortened to gran before both masculine and feminine singular nouns:

un gran señor a great man	una gran señora a great lady

When grande refers to physical size, it usually comes after the noun, in which case it is not shortened:

un coche grande a large car	una cocina grande a large kitchen

c) Cualquiera becomes cualquier before both masculine and feminine singular nouns:

cualquier libro
any book

cualquier casa
any house

The plural of this adjective is cualesquiera. It is seldom used.

d) Santo becomes san before saints' names, except those beginning with either Do- or To-:

San Pablo
San Pedro
Santo Domingo
Santo Tomás

2 Forming the feminine of adjectives

a) Adjectives ending in -o change to -a:

un vuelo corto
a short flight

una estancia corta
a short stay

b) Adjectives ending in other vowels or consonants (other than those in sections c and d) have the same form for both masculine and feminine:

un coche verde
a green car

una hoja verde
a green leaf

un problema fundamental
a fundamental problem

una dificultad fundamental
a fundamental difficulty

c) Those ending in -án, -és, -ín, -ón, and -or add -a:

un niño hablador
a talkative boy

una mujer habladora
a talkative woman

The exceptions are the comparative adjectives ending in -or (*see* page 187):

una idea mejor
a better idea

Note also that those ending in -án, -és, -ín, and -ón lose their accent in the feminine:

una muchacha muy holgazana
a very lazy girl

d) Adjectives indicating nationality or where someone or something comes from add -a if they end in a consonant. Any written accent is also lost:

un hotel escocés	**una pensión escocesa**
a Scottish hotel	a Scottish boarding house
un vino andaluz	**una sopa andaluza**
an Andalusian wine	an Andalusian soup

e) Adjectives ending in -ícola and -ista have the same form for both masculine and feminine:

un país agrícola	**una región vinícola**
an agricultural country	a wine-growing region
el partido comunista	**la ideología socialista**
the communist party	socialist ideology

> Note
>
> There is no separate 'masculine' form for these adjectives. The masculine forms end in **-ista** and **-ícola** like the feminines.

3 The plural of adjectives

Adjectives follow the same rules as nouns for the formation of the plural (*see* pages 173–5):

estos libros son viejos y sucios	**unas personas amables**
these books are old and dirty	some friendly people

The same spelling and accentuation changes also occur:

feliz – felices
holgazán – holgazanes

9 THE COMPARATIVE

For uses of the comparative, see pages 48-52.

1 The standard forms

To form the comparative in Spanish, simply place the word **más** (more), or **menos** (less) before the adjective:

más barato	**más caro**
cheaper	more expensive
menos guapo	**menos feo**
less handsome	less ugly

2 Irregular comparatives

There are six irregular comparatives:

bueno	(good)	→	mejor	(better)
grande	(big)	→	mayor	(bigger)*
malo	(bad)	→	peor	(worse)
mucho	(a lot)	→	más	(more)
pequeño	(small)	→	menor	(smaller)*
poco	(a little)	→	menos	(less)

A number of other adjectives are considered to belong to this group, although their comparative meaning has to some extent been lost:

superior (superior)
inferior (inferior)
anterior (previous)
posterior (rear, subsequent)

* **Más grande** and **más pequeño** exist, but refer rather to physical size. **Mayor** and **menor** refer more to the relative importance of the object or person, or to age.

When referring to age, mayor is often treated in spoken Spanish as a simple adjective meaning 'old', 'grown up' and is sometimes itself put into the comparative:

> **mi hermano más mayor**
> my older brother

Although fairly widespread, this usage is regarded as ungrammatical and should certainly not be imitated in formal written Spanish.

Superior and inferior are widely used with numbers, amounts, quantities *etc*:

> **el paro es superior a tres millones**
> unemployment is in excess of three million

> **los beneficios son inferiores a los del año pasado**
> profits are down on last year's

10 THE SUPERLATIVE

1 The relative superlative

The relative superlative is identical in form to the comparative:

Juan es el estudiante más insolente de la clase
Juan is the most insolent student in class

este coche es el más caro
this car is the dearest

es la peor película que jamás he visto
it's the worst film I've ever seen

2 The absolute superlative

The absolute superlative is formed by adding the ending -ísimo
to the adjective. If the adjective already ends in a vowel, this is
dropped:

alto	→	altísimo
importante	→	importantísimo
fácil	→	facilísimo

When a vowel is dropped from the adjective, spelling changes
may be necessary to ensure that the pronunciation of the absolute
superlative is properly reflected in the spelling of the word:

rico	→	riquísimo
feliz	→	felicísimo
largo	→	larguísimo

Like any other adjective, the relative superlative agrees with the
noun described:

estás guapísima hoy, María
you're looking extremely pretty today, María

estos libros son carísimos
these books are very expensive

11 PREPOSITIONS

A

TO	*destination*	**voy a la escuela/a casa** I am going to school/home
		¿adónde fuiste? where did you go?
AT/IN	*place*	**llega a Madrid mañana** he arrives in Madrid tomorrow
AT/ON	*time*	**comemos a la una** we eat at one o'clock
		se fue a los quince años he left at the age of fifteen
		al día siguiente murió he died (on) the next day
AT/ON	*place where*	**torcieron a la izquierda** they turned to the left
		sentarse a la mesa to sit down at table
ON	*means of transport*	**a pie** **a caballo** on foot on horseback
AT	*cost*	**los vendían a diez euros cada uno** they were selling them at ten euros each
AWAY FROM	*place/time*	**la casa se sitúa a cien metros de aquí** the house is a hundred metres from here
		a los dos días volvió he came back two days later
A	*frequency*	**dos veces al día** twice a day
IN	*opinion*	**a mi ver/a mi juicio/a mis ojos** in my opinion/in my view

| TO | *purpose*
(with verbs of motion) | **fui a comprar pan**
I went to buy bread |
| Personal a | *See page 65* | **he visto a Juan**
I saw Juan |

ANTE

| BEFORE | *in the presence of* | **le llevaron ante el rey**
they brought him before the king |
| | *in the face of* | **ante tanto trabajo huyó**
in the face of so much work he fled |

BAJO

| UNDER (NEATH) | *place* | **construyeron un túnel bajo el mar**
they built a tunnel under the sea |
| | *figuratively* | **bajo el reinado de Felipe II**
under the reign of Philip II |

CON

WITH	*association*	**se fueron con su primo** they left with their cousin
	means	**lo cortó con las tijeras** she cut it with the scissors
TO		**hablaba con su amigo** he was talking to his friend
TOWARDS	*figuratively*	**no seas cruel conmigo** don't be cruel to me

In this last meaning, con is sometimes preceded by para:

era muy amable para con todos
he was very kind to everyone

CONTRA

| AGAINST | *position* | **se apoyaba contra la pared**
he was leaning against the wall |

191

PREPOSITIONS

	opposition	**los rebeldes luchaban contra el gobierno** the rebels were fighting against the government

In this last meaning, the compound preposition **en contra de** is often preferred:

votaron en contra de la ley
they voted against the bill

DE

OF	*material*	**el vestido es de lana** the dress is made of wool
	contents	**un paquete de cigarrillos** a packet of cigarettes
	possession	**es el coche de mi hermana** it's my sister's car
(FOR)	*purpose*	**una cuchara de café** a coffee spoon
FROM	*place*	**es de Londres** he comes from London
		va de Madrid a Salamanca he goes from Madrid to Salamanca
	time	**cenamos de diez a once** we had dinner from ten to eleven
		de año en año vienen aquí they come here year after year
AS	*age*	**se fueron de pequeños** they left as little children
	number	**el peso es de cien kilos** the weight is one hundred kilos
		el total era de mil euros the total was a thousand euros
	cost	**un coche de cinco mil libras** a car costing five thousand pounds

WITH	*descriptions*	**la muchacha de los ojos azules** the girl with the blue eyes
		el señor de la barba the man with the beard
		¡el bobo del niño! the silly boy!
To form adjectival phrases		**la comida de siempre** the usual food
		la parte de fuera the outside part
To form compound prepositions		**además de, alrededor de** *etc.* *See* pages 198–200.

DESDE

FROM	*place*	**le vi llegar desde mi ventana** I saw him arrive from my window
FROM/SINCE	*time*	**toca la guitarra desde niño** he has been playing the guitar since he was a boy

With **hasta**:

FROM … TO/TILL	*time*	**desde las dos hasta las cuatro** from two till four
FROM … TO	*place*	**desde Madrid hasta Barcelona** from Madrid to Barcelona

EN

IN/ON/AT	*position*	**paró en la puerta** he stopped in the doorway
		el ordenador está en la mesa the computer is on the table
		quedarse en casa to stay at home

		los vimos en la Feria de Muestras we saw it at the Exhibition
	opinion	**en mi opinión sería imprudente** in my opinion it would be unwise
INTO	*numbers*	**lo dividió en tres partes** he divided it into three
WITHIN	*time*	**no le he visto en quince días** I haven't seen him in a fortnight
BY	*increase/ decrease*	**los precios han aumentado en un diez por ciento** prices have gone up by ten percent
Phrases		**en balde/en vano** **en seguida** in vain immediately **en absoluto** absolutely not

ENTRE

BETWEEN		**entre la puerta y la pared** between the door and the wall **entre tú y yo** between you and me
AMONG		**lo encontré entre tus papeles** I found it among your papers
TOGETHER		**lo hicimos entre todos** we did it together

HACIA

TOWARDS	*place*	**fue corriendo hacia su padre** he ran towards his father
	figuratively	**muestra hostilidad hacia el jefe** he shows hostility to the boss
ABOUT	*time*	**llegaron hacia las tres** they arrived about three o'clock

HASTA

UNTIL	*time*	**esto continuó hasta el siglo veinte** this continued until the 20th century
UP TO	*number*	**vinieron hasta cien personas** as many as a hundred people turned up
AS FAR AS	*place*	**te acompaño hasta tu casa** I'll walk you home
EVEN	*figuratively*	**hasta los niños quieren acompañarnos** even the children want to come with us

INCLUSO

EVEN	**incluso mi padre está de acuerdo** even my father agrees

MEDIANTE

BY MEANS OF	**lo consiguió mediante mucho trabajo** he achieved it by hard work

PARA

IN ORDER TO	*purpose*	**salió para lavar el coche** he went out to wash the car
		compró una navaja para cortar la cuerda she bought a penknife to cut the rope
		estudió para cura he studied to become a priest
FOR	*in the direction of*	**se fueron para Estados Unidos** they left for the USA
BY	*time by which*	**quiero ese trabajo para mañana** I want that work by tomorrow
		para entonces ya me habré marchado I'll have gone away by then
FOR	*as concerns*	**el cálculo no es difícil para ella** the calculation isn't difficult for her

PREPOSITIONS

FOR	*concession*	**para ser español, habla muy bien inglés** for a Spaniard, he speaks very good English
TO		**siempre murmuraba para sí** she was always muttering to herself
With **estar**	*on the point of*	**estábamos todos para salir** we were all ready to go out
Idioms		**bastante ... para** enough ... to/for
		demasiado ... para too much ... to/for
		suficiente ... para enough ... to/for
		cuesta demasiado para mí it's too expensive for me

POR

BY	*agent*	**el reparo fue terminado por el jefe** the repair was finished by the boss
FOR	*time during*	**habló por dos minutos** he spoke for two minutes
		ocurrió el robo el domingo por la noche the robbery took place on Sunday night
OUT OF		**lo echó por la ventana** she threw it out of the window
THROUGH		**pasaron por Valencia** they went through Valencia
ABOUT	*place*	**rodaron por las cercanías** they roamed about the neighbourhood
		vive por aquí he lives around here
BY/ THROUGH	*means*	**por mí se informaron sobre el desastre** they found out about the disaster through me
		por avión **por teléfono** by air by telephone

IN EXCHANGE FOR		**vendió el coche por cien libras** he sold the car for a hundred pounds
PER/BY	*rate/ sequence*	**cincuenta kilómetros por hora** fifty kilometres per hour
OUT OF/BY	*cause*	**por no estudiar no aprobó el examen** he failed the exam through not having studied
FOR THE SAKE OF/ THROUGH		**por amor le siguió a España** she followed him to Spain out of love
TIMES	*multipli- cation*	**dos por dos son cuatro** two times two are four
FOR	*to get*	**voy a por hielo** I'm going to get some ice
Idioms	tomar ... por	**¿me tomas por idiota?** do you take me for a fool?
	pasar por	**pasa por buen conductor** he is considered a good driver
	estar por	**los platos están por lavar** the dishes still have to be washed
		estoy por salir I feel like going out

SEGÚN

ACCORDING TO	**según él, es peligroso** according to him, it's dangerous
	los precios varían según la época del año prices vary according to the time of year

SIN

WITHOUT	**continuaremos sin su ayuda** we will go on without your help
	sin saber without knowing

PREPOSITIONS

SOBRE

ON/OVER	*place*	**las tazas están sobre la mesa** the cups are on the table
		el avión voló sobre las montañas the plane flew over the mountains
AROUND	*time*	**vendrá sobre las siete** he will come around seven o'clock
ON/ABOUT	*concerning*	**he leído un artículo sobre la guerra** I read an article about the war

TRAS

AFTER	*time*	**tras una reunión de tres horas** after a three hour meeting
	succession	**uno tras otro** one after the other

Compound prepositions

A CAUSA DE	because of	**no salimos a causa de la tormenta** we are not going out because of the storm
A FAVOR DE	in favour of/for	**¿estás a favor de la energía nuclear?** are you in favour of nuclear power?
A FUERZA DE	by (dint of)	**consiguió terminar a fuerza de trabajar noche y día** he managed to finish by dint of working both night and day
A LO LARGO DE	along	**hay flores a lo largo del río** there are flowers all along the riverside
	throughout	**a lo largo del mes de agosto** throughout the month of August
A PESAR DE	in spite of	**salieron a pesar de la lluvia** they went out in spite of the rain

A TRAVÉS DE	across/ through	**la luz entra a través de la ventana** the light comes in through the window
ACERCA DE	about/concerning	**me habló el jefe acerca del empleado** the boss spoke to me about the employee
ADEMÁS DE	besides/as well as	**compré pan además de mantequilla** I bought bread as well as butter
ALREDEDOR DE	about/ around	**gana alrededor de veinte libras al día** he earns around twenty pounds a day
		las casas están situadas alrededor de la iglesia the houses are situated around the church
ANTES DE	before (*time*)	**antes de entrar dejen salir** let people off before getting on
CERCA DE	near	**la casa está cerca del colegio** the house is near the school
	around	**tiene cerca de mil ovejas** he has nearly a thousand sheep
DEBAJO DE	under	**se pararon debajo del árbol** they stopped under the tree
DELANTE DE	in front of	**el coche se detuvo delante del hotel** the car stopped in front of the hotel
DENTRO DE	inside	**encontró un regalo dentro del paquete** she found a gift inside the parcel
DESPUÉS DE	after	**salió después de terminar su trabajo** he went out after finishing his work
		después de las dos after two o'clock
		después de todo after all
DETRÁS DE	behind	**el bar se encuentra detrás del mercado** the bar is behind the market
EN LUGAR DE/ EN VEZ DE	instead of	**en lugar de telefonear, les escribió** instead of phoning, he wrote to them

PREPOSITIONS

EN MEDIO DE	in the middle/ midst of	**paró en medio de tocar la sonata** he stopped in the midst of playing the sonata
ENCIMA DE	on (top of)	**colocó el vaso encima de la mesa** she put the glass on the table
ENFRENTE DE	opposite	**la iglesia está enfrente del Ayuntamiento** the church is opposite the Town Hall
FUERA DE	apart from	**fuera de los de al lado, no conozco a nadie** apart from the next-door neighbours, I don't now anyone
	outside	**la granja está situada fuera de la aldea** the farm is outside the village
LEJOS DE	far from	**la iglesia no está lejos de la escuela** the church is not far from the school
		lejos de acatar la ley far from respecting the law
POR MEDIO DE	by (means of)	**consiguió obtener el dinero por medio de un embuste** he managed to get the money by means of trickery

12 RELATIVE PRONOUNS

For a detailed explanation of the use of relative pronouns, see pages 54-7.

1 Simple relative pronouns

a) que (who, whom, which, that)

Que relates to either persons or things, singular or plural. Note that it is invariable.

b) quien/quienes (who, whom, that)

Quien (singular), quienes (plural) relate exclusively to people and are normally used after prepositions.

2 Compound relative pronouns

The compound relative pronouns have separate forms for masculine singular and plural, and feminine singular and plural. They also have a neuter form (what, which).

a) el que (who, whom, which, that)

	MASCULINE	FEMININE	NEUTER
singular	el que	la que	lo que
plural	los que	las que	

b) el cual (who, whom, which, that)

	MASCULINE	FEMININE	NEUTER
singular	el cual	la cual	lo cual
plural	los cuales	las cuales	

13 PRONOUNS

1 Subject pronouns

	SINGULAR	PLURAL
1st person	yo (I)	nosotros, nosotras (we)
2nd person	tú (you)	vosotros, vosotras (you)
3rd person	él (he, it)	ellos (they)
	ella (she, it)	ellas (they)
	ello (it)	
	usted (you)	ustedes (you)

Usted and ustedes are commonly abbreviated to Vd. and Vds.
(or occasionally to Ud. and Uds.). They are followed by the *third*
person forms of the verb.

*For the difference between Vd. and tú, see pages 60–1. For the use
of ello, see page 60.*

2 Weak object pronouns

For the use of the weak object pronouns, see pages 65–7.

a) Direct object pronouns

	SINGULAR	PLURAL
1st person	me (me)	nos (us)
2nd person	te (you)	os (you)
3rd person	le (him, you)	les (them, you)
	la (her, it, you)	las (them, you)
	lo (it)	los (them)

– le and les are the masculine pronouns used for people;
– lo and los are the masculine pronouns used for things;
– la and las are the feminine pronouns for either people or things.

b) Indirect object pronouns

	SINGULAR	**PLURAL**
1st person	me (to me)	nos (to us)
2nd person	te (to you)	os (to you)
3rd person	le (to him/her/it/you)	les (to them/you)

c) Reflexive pronouns (myself *etc*)

	SINGULAR	**PLURAL**
1st person	me	nos
2nd person	te	os
3rd person	se	se

3 Strong object pronouns

For the use of the strong object pronouns, see page 70.

	SINGULAR	**PLURAL**
1st person	mí	nosotros, nosotras
2nd person	ti	vosotros, vosotras
3rd person	él, ella, ello	ellos, ellas
	Vd.	Vds.
(reflexive)	sí	sí

The pronouns mí, ti and sí combine with con to give the following forms:

conmigo	with me
contigo	with you
consigo	with himself/herself/yourself/themselves/yourselves

4 Position of the pronouns

The weak object pronouns normally come before the verb. In the compound tenses they are placed before the auxiliary verb:

él lo hizo	**yo le he visto**
he did it	I saw him
nos hemos levantado	**Vd. se despierta**
we got up	you wake up

In the following three cases the pronouns come after the verb and are joined to it:

a) when the verb is in the infinitive:

quiero verla	**salió después de hacerlo**
I want to see her	he went out after doing it

However, if the infinitive immediately follows another verb, the pronoun may precede the first verb:

querían encontrarnos
nos querían encontrar
they wanted to meet us

b) when the verb is in the present participle:

estoy pintándolo	**estaba cantándola**
I am painting it	he was singing it

Again, in the case of a progressive form of the verb, the pronoun may precede the first verb:

están llevándolo
lo están llevando
they are carrying it

c) when giving a positive command:

¡déjalo!	**¡date prisa!**
leave it!	hurry up!
¡quédese aquí!	**¡espéreme!**
stay here!	wait for me!

However, the pronoun precedes the verb in a negative command:

¡no lo hagas!
don't do it!

¡no te muevas!
don't move!

5 Changes in accentuation and spelling

a) Accents

Note that when more than one pronoun is added to an infinitive, a present participle or an imperative, a written accent is usually required on the original verb to indicate spoken stress if this has moved to the third last syllable (*see* page 166):

¿quieres pasarme el vino? will you pass me the wine?	¿quieres pasármelo? will you pass me it?
está explicándome la lección he is explaining the lesson to me	está explicándomela he is explaining it to me
dame el libro give me the book	dámelo give me it
ponga el libro en la mesa put the book on the table	póngalo en la mesa put it on the table
	dígame hello (*on the phone*)

b) Changes in spelling

When -se is joined to the verb, any final -s of the verb ending is dropped:

vendámoselo
let's sell it to him

The final -s of the first person plural is dropped before the reflexive pronoun -nos:

sentémonos
let's sit down

The -d of the second person plural imperative is dropped before the reflexive pronoun -os:

sentaos, por favor
have a seat, please

With third conjugation verbs, an accent is then required on the i:

¡vestíos!
get dressed!

The only exception is the verb ir, where the -d of the imperative is in fact retained:

¡idos!
go away!

6 Order of pronouns

When two or more pronouns are being used together they come in the following order:

a) The reflexive se must always come first:

se me ha ocurrido
it occurred to me

se le olvidó
he forgot

b) When a direct and an indirect object pronoun are both being used, the indirect comes first:

me lo dio
he gave me it

nos la mostraron
they showed it to us

c) If there are both a third person direct object pronoun (lo, la, le, los, las, les) and a third person indirect object pronoun (le, les), the indirect **le** and **les** are both replaced by **se** before the direct object pronoun:

se la vendieron (a ella)
they sold it to her

se los mandó (a Vd.)
he sent them to you

The addition of **a él, a ella, a Vd.** or **a Vds.** and the like can clarify to whom the **se** refers.

d) In those cases where the direct object pronouns **me, te, nos** or **os** are used with another indirect object pronoun, the direct object pronoun stands before the verb, and the indirect pronoun is replaced by **a** + the corresponding strong pronoun after the verb:

me mandaron a ti
they sent me to you

nos acercamos a ellos
we approached them

14 ADVERBS

Adverbs are used with verbs, adjectives and other adverbs. When used with a verb, they describe:

– *how* an action is done   adverbs of manner
– *when* an action is done   adverbs of time
– *where* an action is done   adverbs of place
– to what *degree* an action is done   adverbs of degree

1 Adverbs of manner

a) Most of these adverbs can be formed by adding -mente to the feminine singular form of the adjective:

| **lenta** | slow | → | **lentamente** | slowly |
| **extensa** | wide | → | **extensamente** | widely |

Accents appearing on the adjective are retained on the adverb:

| **lógica** | logical | → | **lógicamente** | logically |
| **rápida** | quick | → | **rápidamente** | quickly |

b) When two or more adverbs are used to describe the same verb, only the last one takes -mente, but the initial ones retain the feminine form of the adjective:

caminaron nerviosa y rápidamente
they travelled anxiously and fast

c) The following adverbs of manner do not have a form ending in -mente:

bien	well
mal	badly
adrede	on purpose
así	in this way
despacio	slowly
deprisa	quickly

caminaban despacio por el calor que hacía
they travelled slowly because of the heat

tú has trabajado bien, Juanito
you've done a good job, Juanito

2 Adverbs of time

Most of these adverbs are not formed from adjectives. The commonest are:

ahora	now
anoche	last night
anteanoche	the night before last
anteayer/antes de ayer	the day before yesterday
antes	before
ayer	yesterday
después	after
entonces	then
hoy	today
luego	presently
mañana	tomorrow
nunca	never
pasado mañana	the day after tomorrow
primero	firstly
pronto	soon
prontísimo	very soon
siempre	always
tarde	late
tardísimo	very late
temprano	early
tempranísimo	very early
todavía	still/yet
ya	already/now/presently

Some common adverbial phrases of time:

a continuación	next
acto seguido	immediately after
algunas veces	sometimes
a menudo	often
a veces	sometimes
dentro de poco	soon
de vez en cuando	from time to time
en breve	soon
muchas veces	often
nunca más	never again
otra vez	again
pocas veces	rarely
rara vez	seldom
repetidas veces	again and again
una y otra vez	again and again

quiero empezar ahora, no espero hasta mañana
I want to start now, I'm not waiting until tomorrow

siempre va en tren hasta el centro, luego coge el autobús
she always takes the train into the centre and then catches a bus

quedamos en vernos pasado mañana, no mañana
we agreed to meet the day after tomorrow, not tomorrow

Points to note

a) As well as meaning 'already', ya is used in everyday speech to mean 'right away':

¡ya voy!
I'm coming right away!

There are times when ya has no clear translation into English as it is often used as a filler:

ya me lo decía yo
I thought so

In the negative ya no means 'no longer':

siempre iba a ver a su tía el sábado, pero ya no va
he always used to visit his aunt on Saturdays, but he no longer goes

> *Note*
>
> Do not confuse ya no with todavía no, which means 'not yet':
>
> **todavía no han llegado**
> they haven't arrived yet

b) Luego can also mean 'therefore':

pienso luego existo
I think therefore I am

c) Recientemente is shortened to recién before past participles. Recién
is invariable and does not change its form whatever the gender
or number of the past participle:

una niña recién nacida   **los recién casados**
a new-born baby girl   the newly-weds

3 Adverbs of place

The commonest of these are:

abajo	down/below
ahí/allí	there
allá	over there
aquí	here
arriba	up/above
cerca	near
debajo	below/beneath
delante	forward/in front
dentro	inside
detrás	behind/back
dónde	where

encima	over/above/on
enfrente	opposite
fuera	outside
lejos	far

Some adverbial phrases:

en alguna parte	somewhere
en otra parte	somewhere else
en/por todas partes	everywhere

se me cayeron encima
they fell on me

¿hay alguna tienda por aquí cerca?
is there a shop anywhere around here?

¿dónde está Juan? – está dentro
where's Juan? – he's inside

Points to note

a) Aquí, allí and allá express the same relationships as the demonstrative adjectives este, ese and aquel (*see* page 30):

- aquí   means 'here, near me'
- allí   means 'there, near you'
- allá   means 'there, far from both of us'

b) The forms arriba, abajo, adelante and atrás can be used immediately after a noun in adverbial phrases such as:

andábamos calle abajo
we walked down the street

aquello sucedió años atrás
that event took place years later

Adentro and a través also appear in set phrases:

mar adentro	campo a través
out at sea	cross country

4 Adverbs of degree

The commonest of these are:

algo	somewhat
apenas	hardly
bastante	fairly/rather/enough
casi	almost
como	about
cuánto	how/how much
demasiado	too much
más	more
menos	less
mitad/medio	half
mucho	very much
muy	very much
nada	not at all
poco	little
qué	how
suficientemente	enough
tan	so/as
tanto	so much/as much
todo	entirely
un poco	a little

la casa es muy vieja pero es bastante grande
the house is very old but it is fairly big

me gusta mucho la tortilla, pero no me gustan nada los calamares
I like tortilla very much, but I don't like squid at all

tiene casi tres años, todavía es demasiado pequeño para ir solo
he is almost three, still too little to go by himself

hoy se siente un poco mejor
he is feeling a little better today

Points to note

a) This use of qué is restricted to exclamations:

¡qué inteligente eres!
how clever you are!

b) Muy is used with adjectives and adjectival phrases, and adverbs:

estoy muy cansado   **me parece muy temprano**
I am very tired   it seems very early to me

In a few exceptional cases, it can be used with a noun:

es muy amigo mío
he's a very good friend of mine

When used as an adverb, mucho goes with verbs, comparative adverbs, and comparative adjectives:

me gustó mucho   **está mucho mejor**
I liked it a lot   he's much better

c) When used as an adverb, medio never changes its form:

María estaba medio dormida
María was half asleep

d) Note the common construction with suficientemente:

no es lo suficientemente inteligente como para entender esto
he isn't clever enough to understand this

15 THE VERB

There are three conjugations of verbs in Spanish. The infinitive of a verb indicates which conjugation it belongs to:

– all verbs ending in -ar belong to the first conjugation;
– all verbs ending in -er belong to the second conjugation;
– all verbs ending in -ir belong to the third conjugation.

Some verbs are irregular, and others have minor deviations from the rules. These will be treated separately.

Spanish has many 'radical changing verbs' where changes are made to the stressed vowel of the stem, although the endings of these verbs are perfectly normal. These verbs will be dealt with in a separate section.

All newly coined verbs automatically go into the first conjugation and adopt its endings and forms, eg informatizar (to computerize).

A THE TENSES OF THE INDICATIVE – THE SIMPLE TENSES

Tenses may be either simple – consisting of one word only – or compound, where an auxiliary verb is used with a participle of the main verb.

1 The present tense

The stem for the present tense of the verb is found by removing the endings -ar, -er or -ir from the infinitive. The present tense itself is then formed by adding the following endings to the stem:

1st conjugation	-o, -as, -a, -amos, -áis, -an
2nd conjugation	-o, -es, -e, -emos, -éis, -en
3rd conjugation	-o, -es, -e, -imos, -ís, -en

cant-ar	beb-er	recib-ir
canto	bebo	recibo
cantas	bebes	recibes
canta	bebe	recibe
cantamos	bebemos	recibimos
cantáis	bebéis	recibís
cantan	beben	reciben

Irregularities in the present tense

For ser *and* estar, *and the irregular verbs* haber, dar, ir, tener *and* venir, *see* pages 247-53. *For radical changing verbs, see* pages 232-41.

a) First conjugation verbs ending in -iar and -uar

Most of these verbs have the spoken accent and also a written accent on the final i and u of the stem in all but the first and second persons plural:

enviar	continuar
envío	continúo
envías	continúas
envía	continúa
enviamos	continuamos
enviáis	continuáis
envían	continúan

The commonest exceptions are the verbs cambiar (to change) and averiguar (to ascertain).

b) Second conjugation verbs ending in -ecer

The ending of the first person singular is -ezco. All other forms are regular:

parecer	parezco, pareces ...
crecer	crezco, creces ...

c) Third conjugation verbs ending in -uir, and the verb oír

These verbs add y to the stem *unless* the stem is followed by a stressed i, ie in all but the first and second persons plural. Note that oír also has an irregular first person singular (see below):

construir	oír
construyo	oigo
construyes	oyes
construye	oye
construimos	oímos
construís	oís
construyen	oyen

d) Third conjugation verbs ending in -ucir

The ending of the first person singular is -uzco. All other forms are regular:

conducir	conduzco, conduces ...
producir	produzco, produces ...

e) Second and third conjugation verbs whose stem ends in c or g

Such verbs change the c to z and the g to j in the first person singular. All other forms are regular:

vencer	venzo, vences ...
esparcir	esparzo, esparces ...
escoger	escojo, escoges ...
rugir	rujo, ruges ...

f) Third conjugation verbs whose stem ends in qu or gu

Such verbs change the qu to c and the gu to g in the first person singular. All other forms are regular:

delinquir	delinco, delinques ...
distinguir	distingo, distingues ...

g) Third conjugation verbs whose infinitive ends in -güir

These verbs drop the dieresis except in the first and second persons plural:

argüir	arguyo, arguyes, arguye, argüimos, argüís, arguyen

h) Verbs with an irregular first person singular

The following verbs have largely unpredictable irregularities in the first person singular:

caber	to fit	quepo
caer	to fall	caigo
conocer	to know	conozco
decir	to say	digo
estar	to be	estoy
hacer	to do/make	hago
ir	to go	voy
oír	to hear	oigo
saber	to know	sé
salir	to go out/leave	salgo
ser	to be	soy
tener	to have	tengo
traer	to bring	traigo
valer	to be worth	valgo
venir	to come	vengo

Any compound form of these verbs shares the same irregularities:

contradecir	to contradict	contradigo
obtener	to obtain	obtengo

Note that satisfacer behaves in the same way as hacer:

satisfacer	to satisfy	satisfago

2 The future tense

The future tense of all conjugations is formed by adding the following endings to the infinitive of the verb, irrespective of its conjugation:

> *1st, 2nd & 3rd conjugations* -é, -ás, -á, -emos, -éis, -án

cantaré	beberé	recibiré
cantarás	beberás	recibirás
cantará	beberá	recibirá
cantaremos	beberemos	recibiremos
cantaréis	beberéis	recibiréis
cantarán	beberán	recibirán

Irregularities in the future tense

A number of verbs add these endings to an irregular stem:

caber	to fit	cabré
decir	to say	diré
haber	to have	habré
hacer	to do/make	haré
poder	to be able	podré
poner	to put	pondré
querer	to want	querré
saber	to know	sabré
salir	to go out/leave	saldré
tener	to have	tendré
valer	to be worth	valdré
venir	to come	vendré

Again, any compounds share the same irregularities:

deshacer	to undo	desharé
convenir	to agree/suit	convendré

3 The imperfect tense

The imperfect tense is formed by adding the following endings to the stem of the infinitive:

> *1st conjugation*   -aba, -abas, -aba, -ábamos, -abais, -aban
> *2nd & 3rd conjugations*   -ía, -ías, -ía, -íamos, -íais, -ían

cantaba	bebía	recibía
cantabas	bebías	recibías
cantaba	bebía	recibía
cantábamos	bebíamos	recibíamos
cantabais	bebías	recibíais
cantaban	bebían	recibían

Irregularities in the imperfect tense

There are only three irregular imperfects in Spanish:

ser	ir	ver
era	iba	veía
eras	ibas	veías
era	iba	veía
éramos	íbamos	veíamos
erais	ibais	veíais
eran	iban	veían

4 The preterite tense

The preterite is formed by adding the following endings to the stem of the infinitive:

> *1st conjugation*   -é, -aste, -ó, -amos, -asteis, -aron
> *2nd & 3rd conjugations*   -í, -iste, -ió, -imos, -isteis, -ieron

canté	bebí	recibí
cantaste	bebiste	recibiste
cantó	bebió	recibió
cantamos	bebimos	recibimos
cantasteis	bebisteis	recibisteis
cantaron	bebieron	recibieron

Irregularities in the preterite tense

a) The so-called pretérito grave

This group comprises a sizable number of mostly second and third conjugation verbs which all add the following endings to irregular stems:

-e, -iste, -o, -imos, -isteis, -ieron

Note in particular that the first and third person singular endings are not stressed (the term grave in pretérito grave means 'stressed on the *second last* syllable').

If the stem itself ends in j, the third person plural ending is shortened to -eron.

andar	anduve, anduviste, anduvo, anduvimos, anduvisteis, anduvieron
caber	cupe, cupiste, cupo, cupimos, cupisteis, cupieron
decir	dije, dijiste, dijo, dijimos, dijisteis, dijeron
estar	estuve, estuviste, estuvo, estuvimos, estuvisteis, estuvieron
haber	hube, hubiste, hubo, hubimos, hubisteis, hubieron
hacer	hice, hiciste, hizo, hicimos, hicisteis, hicieron
poder	pude, pudiste, pudo, pudimos, pudisteis, pudieron
poner	puse, pusiste, puso, pusimos, pusisteis, pusieron
querer	quise, quisiste, quiso, quisimos, quisisteis, quisieron
tener	tuve, tuviste, tuvo, tuvimos, tuvisteis, tuvieron
traer	traje, trajiste, trajo, trajimos, trajisteis, trajeron
saber	supe, supiste, supo, supimos, supisteis, supieron
venir	vine, viniste, vino, vinimos, vinisteis, vinieron

All compounds of these verbs share the same irregularities:

contraer	contraje ...
componer	compuse ...

This group also comprises all verbs ending in -ucir, with the exception of lucir, which is regular. Their stem for the preterite ends in uj:

producir	produje, produjiste, produjo, produjimos, produjisteis, produjeron

b) Other verbs

The following verbs are also irregular:

dar	di, diste, dio, dimos, disteis, dieron
ir	fui, fuiste, fue, fuimos, fuisteis, fueron
ser	fui, fuiste, fue, fuimos, fuisteis, fueron
ver	vi, viste, vio, vimos, visteis, vieron

As can be seen, the preterites of ir and ser are identical. However, the context always indicates clearly which one is involved.

c) Spelling changes

First conjugation verbs whose stems end in c or g change these to qu and gu in the first person singular of the preterite. All other forms are regular:

explicar	expliqué, explicaste ...
llegar	llegué, llegaste ...

In verbs ending in -aer, -eer, -oer and -uir, the i of the third person singular and plural ending changes to y. All other forms are regular:

caer	cayó ... cayeron
construir	construyó ... construyeron
leer	leyó ... leyeron
roer	royó ... royeron

The verb oír also belongs to this group:

| oír | oyó ... oyeron |

Third conjugation verbs ending in -güir drop the dieresis in the third persons singular and plural:

| argüir | argüí, argüiste, arguyó, argüimos, argüisteis, arguyeron |

Second and third conjugation verbs whose stems end in ñ drop the i from the third person singular and plural endings:

| gruñir | gruñó ... gruñeron |
| tañer | tañó ... tañeron |

5 The conditional

The conditional is formed for all conjugations by adding the following endings to the infinitive of the verb:

> *1st, 2nd & 3rd conjugations* -ía, -ías, -ía, -íamos, -íais, -ían

cantaría	bebería	recibiría
cantarías	beberías	recibirías
cantaría	bebería	recibiría
cantaríamos	beberíamos	recibiríamos
cantaríais	beberíais	recibiríais
cantarían	beberían	recibirían

Irregularities in the conditional

Any verb with an irregular stem in the future uses the same stem for the formation of the conditional (*see* page 219):

| hacer | haría ... |
| venir | vendría ... |

and so on.

B COMPOUND TENSES

Compound tenses are formed by using an auxiliary verb with either the present or the past participle.

1 The present participle

a) The regular forms

The present participle is formed by adding the following endings to the stem of the infinitive:

> *1st conjugation*   -ando
> *2nd & 3rd conjugations*   -iendo

b) Irregular present participles

In verbs ending in -aer, -eer, -oer and -uir, and the verb oír, the i of the ending is changed to y:

caer	cayendo
construir	construyendo
creer	creyendo
oír	oyendo
roer	royendo

Verbs ending in -güir drop the dieresis in the present participle:

argüir	arguyendo

Second and third conjugation verbs whose stems end in ñ drop the i from the ending:

gruñir	gruñendo
tañer	tañendo

Third conjugation radical changing verbs of groups 3, 4 and 5 also have irregular present participles (*see* **pages 235-9**):

dormir	durmiendo

pedir	pidiendo
sentir	sintiendo

2 The past participle

a) The regular forms

To form the past participle of a regular verb remove the infinitive ending and add:

1st conjugation	-ado	**cantado**
2nd & 3rd conjugations	-ido	**bebido, recibido**

b) Irregular past participles

Some verbs have irregular past participles. The most common are:

abrir	to open	**abierto**	opened
cubrir	to cover	**cubierto**	covered
decir	to say	**dicho**	said
escribir	to write	**escrito**	written
hacer	to make/do	**hecho**	made/done
morir	to die	**muerto**	dead
poner	to put	**puesto**	put
resolver	to solve	**resuelto**	solved
ver	to see	**visto**	seen
volver	to return	**vuelto**	returned

Compounds of these verbs have the same irregularities in their past participles, eg:

descubrir	to discover	**des**cubierto	discovered
describir	to describe	**des**crito	described

The verb satisfacer behaves in the same way as hacer:

satisfacer	to satisfy	**satis**fecho	satisfied

3 The progressive forms of the tenses

A progressive form of any tense can be formed by using estar (or one of an associated group of verbs) with the present participle.

For the full conjugation of estar, *see* page 248:

estamos trabajando
we are working

yo estaba estudiando cuando Juan entró
I was studying when Juan came in

For a full discussion of the progressive tenses, see pages 81-83.

4 The perfect tense

The compound past tenses are formed with the appropriate tense of the verb haber together with the past participle of the verb.

For the full conjugation of haber, *see* page 249.

The perfect tense is formed by using the present tense of haber with the past participle of the main verb:

he cantado	he bebido	he recibido
has cantado	has bebido	has recibido
ha cantado	ha bebido	ha recibido
hemos cantado	hemos bebido	hemos recibido
habéis cantado	habéis bebido	habéis recibido
han cantado	han bebido	han recibido

5 The pluperfect tense

The pluperfect tense is formed by using the imperfect of haber with the past participle of the main verb:

había cantado	había bebido	había recibido
habías cantado	habías bebido	habías recibido
había cantado	había bebido	había recibido
habíamos cantado	habíamos bebido	habíamos recibido
habíais cantado	habíais bebido	habíais recibido
habían cantado	habían bebido	habían recibido

6 The future perfect tense

The future perfect tense is formed by using the future of haber with the past participle of the main verb:

habré cantado	habré bebido	habré recibido
habrás cantado	habrás bebido	habrás recibido
habrá cantado	habrá bebido	habrá recibido
habremos cantado	habremos bebido	habremos recibido
habréis cantado	habréis bebido	habréis recibido
habrán cantado	habrán bebido	habrán recibido

7 The past anterior tense

The past anterior tense is formed by using the preterite of haber with the past participle of the main verb:

hube cantado	hube bebido	hube recibido
hubiste cantado	hubiste bebido	hubiste recibido
hubo cantado	hubo bebido	hubo recibido
hubimos cantado	hubimos bebido	hubimos recibido
hubisteis cantado	hubisteis bebido	hubisteis recibido
hubieron cantado	hubieron bebido	hubieron recibido

8 The conditional perfect

The conditional perfect is formed by using the conditional of haber with the past participle of the main verb:

habría cantado	habría bebido	habría recibido
habrías cantado	habrías bebido	habrías recibido
habría cantado	habría bebido	habría recibido
habríamos cantado	habríamos bebido	habríamos recibido
habríais cantado	habríais bebido	habríais recibido
habrían cantado	habrían bebido	habrían recibido

C THE TENSES OF THE SUBJUNCTIVE MOOD

1 The present subjunctive

With the exception of a few irregular verbs (estar, ser, ir, dar) the stem for the present subjunctive of a verb is found by removing the -o from the ending of the first person singular of the present tense. The subjunctive is then formed by adding the following endings to that stem.

1st conjugation	-e, -es, -e, -emos, -éis, -en
2nd & 3rd conjugations	-a, -as, -a, -amos, -áis, -an

cant-o	beb-o	recib-o
cante	beba	reciba
cantes	bebas	recibas
cante	beba	reciba
cantemos	bebamos	recibamos
cantéis	bebáis	recibáis
canten	beban	reciban

Irregularities in the present subjunctive

(For radical changing verbs, see pages 232–41.*)*

a) Verbs ending in -iar and -uar

  Such verbs have the same pattern of accentuation in the subjunctive as they do in the indicative, ie a written accent on the i or u of the stem in all but the first and second persons plural:

enviar	envíe, envíes, envíe, enviemos, enviéis, envíen
continuar	continúe, continúes, continúe, continuemos, continuéis, continúen

b) Irregular stems

Since the stem of the subjunctive is based on the first person singular of the indicative, any irregularities there appear throughout the present subjunctive, for example:

infinitive	*1st pers. pres.*	*subjunctive*
coger	cojo	coja, cojas, coja, cojamos, cojáis, cojan
decir	digo	diga, digas, diga, digamos, digáis, digan
parecer	parezco	parezca, parezcas, parezca, parezcamos, parezcáis, parezcan
poner	pongo	ponga, pongas, ponga, pongamos, pongáis, pongan
vencer	venzo	venza, venzas, venza, venzamos, venzáis, venzan

c) Spelling changes

buscar	busque, busques, busque, busquemos, busquéis, busquen
llegar	llegue, llegues, llegue, lleguemos, lleguéis, lleguen

First conjugation verbs ending in -guar require a dieresis throughout the present subjunctive.

averiguar	averigüe, averigües, averigüe, averigüemos, averigüéis, averigüen

2 The imperfect subjunctive

The stem for the imperfect subjunctive is found by removing the ending -ron from the third person plural of the preterite of the verb. The imperfect subjunctive has two possible forms, formed by adding the following endings to that stem:

1st conjugation	-ara, -aras, -ara, -áramos, -arais, -aran
	-ase, -ases, -ase, -ásemos, -aseis, -asen
2nd & 3rd conjugations	-iera, -ieras, -iera, -iéramos, -ierais, -ieran
	-iese, -ieses, -iese, -iésemos, -ieseis, -iesen

cantara/cantase	bebiera/bebiese	recibiera/recibiese
cantaras/cantases	bebieras/bebieses	recibieras/recibieses
cantara/cantase	bebiera/bebiese	recibiera/recibiese
cantáramos/ cantásemos	bebiéramos/ bebiésemos	recibiéramos/ recibiésemos
cantarais/cantaseis	bebierais/bebieseis	recibierais/recibieseis
cantaran/cantasen	bebieran/bebiesen	recibieran/recibiesen

In general, the first form of each pair is more common in spoken Spanish.

Verbs whose preterites are irregular display the same irregularity in the imperfect subjunctive:

infinitive	*preterite*	*imperfect subjunctive*
decir	dijeron	dijera/dijese
tener	tuvieron	tuviera/tuviese
venir	vinieron	viniera/viniese

Compounds of these verbs display the same irregularities:

convenir	conviniera/conviniese
obtener	obtuviera/obtuviese

3 The perfect subjunctive

The perfect tense of the subjunctive is formed by using the present subjunctive of haber with the past participle of the main verb:

haya cantado	haya bebido	haya recibido
hayas cantado	hayas bebido	hayas recibido
haya cantado	haya bebido	haya recibido
hayamos cantado	hayamos bebido	hayamos recibido
hayáis cantado	hayáis bebido	hayáis recibido
hayan cantado	hayan bebido	hayan recibido

4 The pluperfect subjunctive

The pluperfect of the subjunctive is formed by using the imperfect subjunctive of haber with the past participle of the main verb:

hubiera cantado	hubiera bebido	hubiera recibido
hubieras cantado	hubieras bebido	hubieras recibido
hubiera cantado	hubiera bebido	hubiera recibido
hubiéramos cantado	hubiéramos bebido	hubiéramos recibido
hubierais cantado	hubierais bebido	hubierais recibido
hubieran cantado	hubieran bebido	hubieran recibido

hubiese cantado	hubiese bebido	hubiese recibido
hubieses cantado	hubieses bebido	hubieses recibido
hubiese cantado	hubiese bebido	hubiese recibido
hubiésemos cantado	hubiésemos bebido	hubiésemos recibido
hubieseis cantado	hubieseis bebido	hubieseis recibido
hubiesen cantado	hubiesen bebido	hubiesen recibido

D THE IMPERATIVE

The imperative proper exists only for the tú and vosotros forms of the verb, and is used *only* in positive commands. It is formed as follows:

tú	*All conjugations*: remove the -s from the second person singular of the present indicative of the verb.
vosotros	*First and second conjugations*: remove the -áis/-éis from the second person plural of the present indicative of the verb and replace it with -ad/-ed.
	Third conjugation: remove the -ís from the second person plural of the present indicative of the verb and replace it with -id.

hablar	habla	hablad
comer	come	comed
escribir	escribe	escribid

Note that, since the tú form is based on the second person singular of the verb, any radical changes will also be present in the singular, but not in the plural form of the imperative:

cerrar	cierra	cerrad
torcer	tuerce	torced
pedir	pide	pedid

There are a number of irregular imperatives in the tú form:

decir	di	decid
hacer	haz	haced
ir	ve	id
poner	pon	poned
salir	sal	salid
ser	sé	sed *(also irregular in plural)*
tener	ten	tened
valer	val	valed
venir	ven	venid

Commands addressed to all other persons – Vd., Vds., third and first person (ie 'let's') commands – and *all* negative commands are formed using the subjunctive. *See* **pages 76-7** *for details.*

E THE RADICAL CHANGING VERBS

Some verbs have spelling changes to their stem when the latter is stressed. The endings are not affected unless the verb itself is irregular.

1 e changes to ie (first and second conjugations only)

The commonest of these verbs are:

acertar	to guess correctly
alentar	to encourage
apretar	to squeeze
ascender	to go up, to come to

atender	to attend to
aterrar	to terrify
atravesar	to cross
calentar	to heat
cerrar	to close
comenzar	to begin
concertar	to agree to
condescender	to condescend
confesar	to confess
defender	to defend
desalentar	to discourage
desatender	to disregard
descender	to come down
desconcertar	to disconcert
despertar	to waken
desplegar	to unfold
discernir	to discern
empezar	to begin
encender	to light, to switch on
encerrar	to enclose
encomendar	to entrust
entender	to understand
enterrar	to bury
extender	to extend
fregar	to scrub
gobernar	to govern
helar	to freeze
manifestar	to show
merendar	to have tea
negar	to deny
nevar	to snow
pensar	to think
perder	to lose
quebrar	to break

recomendar	to recommend
regar	to irrigate
reventar	to burst
sembrar	to sow
sentarse	to sit
sosegar	to calm
temblar	to tremble
tender	to stretch out
tener*	to have
tentar	to attempt
tropezar	to stumble
verter	to pour

The change occurs in the present indicative and the present subjunctive only, wherever the **e** is stressed, ie the three persons of the singular and the third person plural:

present indicative	*present subjunctive*
atravieso	atraviese
atraviesas	atravieses
atraviesa	atraviese
atravesamos	atravesemos
atravesáis	atraveséis
atraviesan	atraviesen

Note that if the stressed **e** is the first letter in the word, it changes to **ye** and not **ie**:

errar to wander   yerro, yerras, yerra, erramos, erráis, yerran

* Tener has an irregular first person singular: **tengo**. The subjunctive of tener is based on this irregular first person singular:

tenga, tengas, tenga, tengamos, tengáis, tengan

2 o changes to ue (first and second conjugations only)

The commonest verbs in this group are:

absolver	to absolve
acordarse	to remember
acostarse	to go to bed
almorzar	to lunch
apostar	to bet
aprobar	to approve
avergonzarse	to be ashamed
cocer	to cook
colarse	to slip in
colgar	to hang
comprobar	to check
concordar	to agree
conmover	to move
consolar	to console
contar	to count, to tell
costar	to cost
demostrar	to demonstrate
desaprobar	to disapprove
descolgar	to take down
descontar	to deduct
desenvolverse	to get by
despoblar	to depopulate
devolver	to give back
disolver	to dissolve
doler	to hurt
encontrar	to meet, to find
envolver	to wrap
esforzarse	to endeavour
forzar	to force
holgar	to be idle
jugar*	to play
llover	to rain
moler	to grind
morder	to bite

mostrar	to show
mover	to move
oler**	to smell
probar	to try, to taste
promover	to promote
recordar	to remember
renovar	to renew
resollar	to wheeze
resolver	to resolve
resonar	to resound
revolver	to revolve
rodar	to prowl
rogar	to ask
soldar	to weld
soler	to be in the habit of
soltar	to let go
sonar	to ring, to sound
soñar	to dream
torcer	to twist, to turn
tostar	to toast
trocar	to exchange
tronar	to thunder
volar	to fly
volcar	to tip over
volver	to return

The pattern of change is identical to that of group 1:

present indicative	*present subjunctive*
vuelvo	vuelva
vuelves	vuelvas
vuelve	vuelva
volvemos	volvamos
volvéis	volváis
vuelven	vuelvan

* Jugar: the u changes to ue when stressed: juego.

** Oler: h is added to all forms where the change occurs: huele *etc.*

3 e changes to ie and i (third conjugation only)

The commonest verbs in this group are:

adherir	to join
adquirir*	to acquire
advertir	to notice
arrepentirse	to repent
asentir	to agree
conferir	to confer
consentir	to agree
convertir	to convert
digerir	to digest
divertir	to amuse
erguir**	to raise
herir	to wound
hervir	to boil
inferir	to infer
inquirir*	to enquire into
invertir	to invest
mentir	to tell lies
pervertir	to pervert
preferir	to prefer
presentir	to foresee
proferir	to utter
referir	to refer
requerir	to require
resentirse	to resent
sentir	to feel
subvertir	to subvert
sugerir	to suggest
transferir	to transfer
venir***	to come

When stressed, **e** changes to **ie** in the present indicative, present subjunctive, and imperative singular.

Also, unstressed **e** changes to **i** in:

– the 1st and 2nd persons plural of the present subjunctive;
– the present participle;
– the 3rd persons singular and plural of the preterite;
– all of the imperfect subjunctive.

present	*preterite*
siento	sentí
sientes	sentiste
siente	sintió
sentimos	sentimos
sentís	sentisteis
sienten	sintieron

present subjunctive	*imperfect subjunctive*
sienta	sintiera/sintiese
sientas	sintieras/sintieses
sienta	sintiera/sintiese
sintamos	sintiéramos/sintiésemos
sintáis	sintierais/sintieseis
sientan	sintieran/sintiesen

imperative	*present participle*
siente	sintiendo

* In the case of **adquirir** and **inquirir** it is the **i** of the stem which changes to **ie**.

** When stressed, the **e** of **erguir** changes to **ye** and not **ie**:

yergo, yergues, yergue, erguimos, erguís, yerguen

*** **Venir** has an irregular first person singular: **vengo**. The subjunctive of **venir** is based on this irregular first person singular:

venga, vengas, venga, vengamos, vengáis, vengan

4 e changes to i (third conjugation only)

The commonest verbs in this group are:

colegir	to collect
competir	to compete
concebir	to design
conseguir	to manage
corregir	to correct
derretir	to melt
despedir	to sack
elegir	to elect
expedir	to dispatch
gemir	to groan
impedir	to prevent
invertir	to invest
medir	to measure
pedir	to ask for
perseguir	to persecute
proseguir	to continue
regir	to govern
rendir	to yield
repetir	to repeat
seguir	to follow
servir	to serve
vestir	to dress

When stressed, e changes to i in the present indicative, present subjunctive, and imperative singular.

Also, unstressed e changes to i in:

- the 1st and 2nd persons plural of the present subjunctive;
- the present participle;
- the 3rd persons singular and plural of the preterite;
- all of the imperfect subjunctive.

present	*preterite*
pido	pedí
pides	pediste
pide	pidió
pedimos	pedimos
pedís	pedisteis
piden	pidieron

present subjunctive	*imperfect subjunctive*
pida	pidiera/pidiese
pidas	pidieras/pidieses
pida	pidiera/pidiese
pidamos	pidiéramos/pidiésemos
pidáis	pidierais/pidiesais
pidan	pidieran/pidiesen

imperative	*present participle*
pide	pidiendo

Verbs in this group which end in -eír and -eñir make an additional
change: if the ending begins with an unstressed i, this i is
dropped if it comes immediately after the ñ or i of the stem. This
occurs only in the present participle, the third persons singular
and plural of the preterite, and in the imperfect subjunctive.
The commonest verbs in this group are:

ceñir	to fit closely
desteñir	to fade
freír	to fry
reír	to laugh
reñir	to scold
sonreír	to smile
teñir	to dye
reír	ceñir
riendo	ciñendo
rio	ciñó
rieron	ciñeron

5 o changes to ue and u (third conjugation only)

The pattern of changes is identical to that of group 3 above. In other words:

When stressed, o changes to ue in the present indicative, present subjunctive, and imperative singular.

Unstressed o changes to u in:

– the 1st and 2nd persons plural of the present subjunctive;
– the present participle;
– the 3rd persons singular and plural of the preterite;
– all of the imperfect subjunctive.

The commonest verbs in this group are dormir (to sleep) and morir (to die) and their compounds.

present	*preterite*
duermo	dormí
duermes	dormiste
duerme	durmió
dormimos	dormimos
dormís	dormisteis
duermen	durmieron

present subjunctive	*imperfect subjunctive*
duerma	durmiera/durmiese
duermas	durmieras/durmieses
duerma	durmiera/durmiese
durmamos	durmiéramos/durmiésemos
durmáis	durmierais/durmieseis
duerman	durmieran/durmiesen

imperative	*present participle*
duerme	durmiendo

F CONJUGATION TABLES

The following verb tables provide the main conjugation patterns,
including the conjugation of the most common irregular verbs:

-ar verbs	(*see* page 215)	HABLAR
-er verbs	(*see* page 215)	COMER
-ir verbs	(*see* page 215)	VIVIR
Reflexive verbs	(*see* pages 74-5)	BAÑARSE
Auxiliaries	(*see* pages 105-9)	SER
	(*see* pages 105-9)	ESTAR
	(*see* page 114)	HABER
Common irregular verbs		DAR
		IR
		TENER
		VENIR

'Chambers Spanish Verbs', a fully comprehensive list of Spanish
verbs and their conjugations, is also available in this series.

HABLAR *to speak*

PRESENT	IMPERFECT	FUTURE
1. hablo	hablaba	hablaré
2. hablas	hablabas	hablarás
3. habla	hablaba	hablará
1. hablamos	hablábamos	hablaremos
2. habláis	hablabais	hablaréis
3. hablan	hablaban	hablarán

PRETERITE	PERFECT	PLUPERFECT
1. hablé	he hablado	había hablado
2. hablaste	has hablado	habías hablado
3. habló	ha hablado	había hablado
1. hablamos	hemos hablado	habíamos hablado
2. hablasteis	habéis hablado	habíais hablado
3. hablaron	han hablado	habían hablado

PAST ANTERIOR	FUTURE PERFECT
hube hablado *etc*	habré hablado *etc*

CONDITIONAL

		IMPERATIVE

PRESENT	PAST	
1. hablaría	habría hablado	
2. hablarías	habrías hablado	(tú) habla
3. hablaría	habría hablado	(Vd) hable
1. hablaríamos	habríamos hablado	(nosotros) hablemos
2. hablaríais	habríais hablado	(vosotros) hablad
3. hablarían	habrían hablado	(Vds) hablen

SUBJUNCTIVE

PRESENT	IMPERFECT	PLUPERFECT
1. hable	habl-ara/ase	hubiera hablado
2. hables	habl-aras/ases	hubieras hablado
3. hable	habl-ara/ase	hubiera hablado
1. hablemos	habl-áramos/ásemos	hubiéramos hablado
2. habléis	habl-arais/aseis	hubierais hablado
3. hablen	habl-aran/asen	hubieran hablado

PERFECT
haya hablado *etc*

INFINITIVE

	PARTICIPLE

PRESENT	PRESENT
hablar	hablando

PAST	PAST
haber hablado	hablado

COMER *to eat*

PRESENT	IMPERFECT	FUTURE
1. como	comí	comeré
2. comes	comías	comerás
3. come	comía	comerá
1. comemos	comíamos	comeremos
2. coméis	comíais	comeréis
3. comen	comían	comerán

PRETERITE	PERFECT	PLUPERFECT
1. comí	he comido	había comido
2. comiste	has comido	habías comido
3. comió	ha comido	había comido
1. comimos	hemos comido	habíamos comido
2. comisteis	habéis comido	habíais comido
3. comieron	han comido	habían comido

PAST ANTERIOR	FUTURE PERFECT
hube comido *etc*	habré comido *etc*

CONDITIONAL

IMPERATIVE

PRESENT	PAST	
1. comería	habría comido	
2. comerías	habrías comido	(tú) come
3. comería	habría comido	(Vd) coma
1. comeríamos	habríamos comido	(nosotros) comamos
2. comeríais	habríais comido	(vosotros) comed
3. comerían	habrían comido	(Vds) coman

SUBJUNCTIVE

PRESENT	IMPERFECT	PLUPERFECT
1. coma	com-iera/iese	hubiera comido
2. comas	com-ieras/ieses	hubieras comido
3. coma	com-iera/iese	hubiera comido
1. comamos	com-iéramos/iésemos	hubiéramos comido
2. comáis	com-ierais/ieseis	hubierais comido
3. coman	com-ieran/iesen	hubieran comido

PERFECT
haya comido *etc*

INFINITIVE

PARTICIPLE

PRESENT	PRESENT
comer	comiendo
PAST	**PAST**
haber comido	comido

VIVIR *to live*

PRESENT	IMPERFECT	FUTURE
1. vivo	vivía	viviré
2. vives	vivías	vivirás
3. vive	vivía	vivirá
1. vivimos	vivíamos	viviremos
2. vivís	vivíais	viviréis
3. viven	vivían	vivirán

PRETERITE	PERFECT	PLUPERFECT
1. viví	he vivido	había vivido
2. viviste	has vivido	habías vivido
3. vivió	ha vivido	había vivido
1. vivimos	hemos vivido	habíamos vivido
2. vivisteis	habéis vivido	habíais vivido
3. vivieron	han vivido	habían vivido

PAST ANTERIOR		FUTURE PERFECT
hube vivido *etc*		habré vivido *etc*

CONDITIONAL

IMPERATIVE

PRESENT	PAST	
1. viviría	habría vivido	
2. vivirías	habrías vivido	(tú) vive
3. viviría	habría vivido	(Vd) viva
1. viviríamos	habríamos vivido	(nosotros) vivamos
2. viviríais	habríais vivido	(vosotros) vivid
3. vivirían	habrían vivido	(Vds) vivan

SUBJUNCTIVE

PRESENT	IMPERFECT	PLUPERFECT
1. viva	viv-iera/iese	hubiera vivido
2. vivas	viv-ieras/ieses	hubieras vivido
3. viva	viv-iera/iese	hubiera vivido
1. vivamos	viv-iéramos/iésemos	hubiéramos vivido
2. viváis	viv-ierais/ieseis	hubierais vivido
3. vivan	viv-ieran/iesen	hubieran vivido

PERFECT		
haya vivido *etc*		

INFINITIVE

PARTICIPLE

PRESENT	PRESENT
vivir	viviendo
PAST	PAST
haber vivido	vivido

BAÑARSE *to have a bath*

PRESENT	IMPERFECT	FUTURE
1. me baño	me bañaba	me bañaré
2. te bañas	te bañabas	te bañarás
3. se baña	se bañaba	se bañará
1. nos bañamos	nos bañábamos	nos bañaremos
2. os bañáis	os bañabais	os bañaréis
3. se bañan	se bañaban	se bañarán

PRETERITE	PERFECT	PLUPERFECT
1. me bañé	me he bañado	me había bañado
2. te bañaste	te has bañado	te habías bañado
3. se bañó	se ha bañado	se había bañado
1. nos bañamos	nos hemos bañado	nos habíamos bañado
2. os bañasteis	os habéis bañado	os habíais bañado
3. se bañaron	se han bañado	se habían bañado

PAST ANTERIOR	FUTURE PERFECT
me hube bañado *etc*	me habré bañado *etc*

CONDITIONAL

IMPERATIVE

PRESENT	PAST	
1. me bañaría	me habría bañado	
2. te bañarías	te habrías bañado	(tú) báñate
3. se bañaría	se habría bañado	(Vd) báñese
1. nos bañaríamos	nos habríamos bañado	(nosotros) bañémonos
2. os bañaríais	os habríais bañado	(vosotros) bañaos
3. se bañarían	se habrían bañado	(Vds) báñense

SUBJUNCTIVE

PRESENT	IMPERFECT	PLUPERFECT
1. me bañe	me bañ-ara/ase	me hubiera bañado
2. te bañes	te bañ-aras/ases	te hubieras bañado
3. se bañe	se bañ-ara/ase	se hubiera bañado
1. nos bañemos	nos bañ-áramos/ásemos	nos hubiéramos bañado
2. os bañéis	os bañ-arais/aseis	os hubierais bañado
3. se bañen	se bañ-aran/asen	se hubieran bañado

PERFECT
me haya bañado *etc*

INFINITIVE

PARTICIPLE

PRESENT	PRESENT
bañarse	bañándose
PAST	**PAST**
haberse bañado	bañado

SER *to be*

PRESENT	IMPERFECT	FUTURE
1. soy	era	seré
2. eres	eras	serás
3. es	era	será
1. somos	éramos	seremos
2. sois	erais	seréis
3. son	eran	serán

PRETERITE	PERFECT	PLUPERFECT
1. fui	he sido	había sido
2. fuiste	has sido	habías sido
3. fue	ha sido	había sido
1. fuimos	hemos sido	habíamos sido
2. fuisteis	habéis sido	habíais sido
3. fueron	han sido	habían sido

PAST ANTERIOR	FUTURE PERFECT
hube sido *etc*	habré sido *etc*

CONDITIONAL · IMPERATIVE

PRESENT	PAST	IMPERATIVE
1. sería	habría sido	
2. serías	habrías sido	(tú) **sé**
3. sería	habría sido	(Vd) sea
1. seríamos	habríamos sido	(nosotros) seamos
2. seríais	habríais sido	(vosotros) sed
3. serían	habrían sido	(Vds) sean

SUBJUNCTIVE

PRESENT	IMPERFECT	PLUPERFECT
1. sea	fu-era/ese	hubiera sido
2. seas	fu-eras/eses	hubieras sido
3. sea	fu-era/ese	hubiera sido
1. seamos	fu-éramos/ésemos	hubiéramos sido
2. seáis	fu-erais/eseis	hubierais sido
3. sean	fu-eran/esen	hubieran sido

PERFECT
haya sido *etc*

INFINITIVE · PARTICIPLE

INFINITIVE	PARTICIPLE
PRESENT	PRESENT
ser	siendo
PAST	PAST
haber sido	sido

ESTAR *to be*

PRESENT	IMPERFECT	FUTURE
1. estoy	estaba	estaré
2. estás	estabas	estarás
3. está	estaba	estará
1. estamos	estábamos	estaremos
2. estáis	estabais	estaréis
3. están	estaban	estarán

PRETERITE	PERFECT	PLUPERFECT
1. estuve	he estado	había estado
2. estuviste	has estado	habías estado
3. estuvo	ha estado	había estado
1. estuvimos	hemos estado	habíamos estado
2. estuvisteis	habéis estado	habíais estado
3. estuvieron	han estado	habían estado

PAST ANTERIOR		FUTURE PERFECT
hube estado *etc*		habré estado *etc*

CONDITIONAL

IMPERATIVE

PRESENT	PAST	
1. estaría	habría estado	
2. estarías	habrías estado	(tú) está
3. estaría	habría estado	(Vd) esté
1. estaríamos	habríamos estado	(nosotros) estemos
2. estaríais	habríais estado	(vosotros) estad
3. estarían	habrían estado	(Vds) estén

SUBJUNCTIVE

PRESENT	IMPERFECT	PLUPERFECT
1. esté	estuv-iera/iese	hubiera estado
2. estés	estuv-ieras/ieses	hubieras estado
3. esté	estuv-iera/iese	hubiera estado
1. estemos	estuv-iéramos/iésemos	hubiéramos estado
2. estéis	estuv-ierais/ieseis	hubierais estado
3. estén	estuv-ieran/iesen	hubieran estado

PERFECT
haya estado *etc*

INFINITIVE

PARTICIPLE

PRESENT	PRESENT
estar	estando
PAST	**PAST**
haber estado	estado

HABER *to have (auxiliary)*

PRESENT	IMPERFECT	FUTURE
1. he	había	habré
2. has	habías	habrás
3. ha/hay*	había	habrá
1. hemos	habíamos	habremos
2. habéis	habíais	habréis
3. han	habían	habrán

PRETERITE	PERFECT	PLUPERFECT
1. hube		
2. hubiste		
3. hubo	ha habido	había habido
1. hubimos		
2. hubisteis		
3. hubieron		

PAST ANTERIOR	FUTURE PERFECT
hubo habido *etc*	habrá habido *etc*

CONDITIONAL

IMPERATIVE

PRESENT	PAST
1. habría	
2. habrías	
3. habría	habría habido
1. habríamos	
2. habríais	
3. habrían	

SUBJUNCTIVE

PRESENT	IMPERFECT	PLUPERFECT
1. haya	hub-iera/iese	
2. hayas	hub-ieras/ieses	
3. haya	hub-iera/iese	hubiera habido
1. hayamos	hub-iéramos/iésemos	
2. hayáis	hub-ierais/ieseis	
3. hayan	hub-ieran/iesen	

PERFECT
haya habido *etc*

INFINITIVE	PARTICIPLE	NOTE
PRESENT	PRESENT	This verb is an auxiliary used
haber	habiendo	for compound tenses (eg he
PAST	PAST	bebido – I have drunk)
haber habido	habido	*hay means 'there is/are'.

DAR *to give*

PRESENT	IMPERFECT	FUTURE
1. doy	daba	daré
2. das	dabas	darás
3. da	daba	dará
1. damos	dábamos	daremos
2. dais	dabais	daréis
3. dan	daban	darán

PRETERITE	PERFECT	PLUPERFECT
1. di	he dado	había dado
2. diste	has dado	habías dado
3. dio	ha dado	había dado
1. dimos	hemos dado	habíamos dado
2. disteis	habéis dado	habíais dado
3. dieron	han dado	habían dado

PAST ANTERIOR	FUTURE PERFECT
hube dado *etc*	habré dado *etc*

CONDITIONAL

IMPERATIVE

PRESENT	PAST	
1. daría	habría dado	
2. darías	habrías dado	(tú) da
3. daría	habría dado	(Vd) dé
1. daríamos	habríamos dado	(nosotros) demos
2. daríais	habríais dado	(vosotros) dad
3. darían	habrían dado	(Vds) den

SUBJUNCTIVE

PRESENT	IMPERFECT	PLUPERFECT
1. dé	di-era/ese	hubiera dado
2. des	di-eras/eses	hubieras dado
3. dé	di-era/ese	hubiera dado
1. demos	di-éramos/ésemos	hubiéramos dado
2. deis	di-erais/eseis	hubierais dado
3. den	di-eran/esen	hubieran dado

PERFECT
haya dado *etc*

INFINITIVE

PARTICIPLE

PRESENT	PRESENT
dar	dando
PAST	**PAST**
haber dado	dado

IR *to go*

PRESENT	IMPERFECT	FUTURE
1. voy	iba	iré
2. vas	ibas	irás
3. va	iba	irá
1. vamos	íbamos	iremos
2. vais	ibais	iréis
3. van	iban	irán

PRETERITE	PERFECT	PLUPERFECT
1. fui	he ido	había ido
2. fuiste	has ido	habías ido
3. fue	ha ido	había ido
1. fuimos	hemos ido	habíamos ido
2. fuisteis	habéis ido	habíais ido
3. fueron	han ido	habían ido

PAST ANTERIOR	FUTURE PERFECT
hube ido *etc*	habré ido *etc*

CONDITIONAL / IMPERATIVE

PRESENT	PAST	IMPERATIVE
1. iría	habría ido	
2. irías	habrías ido	(tú) **ve**
3. iría	habría ido	(Vd) **vaya**
1. iríamos	habríamos ido	(nosotros) **vamos**
2. iríais	habríais ido	(vosotros) **id**
3. irían	habrían ido	(Vds) **vayan**

SUBJUNCTIVE

PRESENT	IMPERFECT	PLUPERFECT
1. vaya	fu-era/ese	hubiera ido
2. vayas	fu-eras/eses	hubieras ido
3. vaya	fu-era/ese	hubiera ido
1. vayamos	fu-éramos/ésemos	hubiéramos ido
2. vayáis	fu-erais/eseis	hubierais ido
3. vayan	fu-eran/esen	hubieran ido

PERFECT
haya ido *etc*

INFINITIVE / PARTICIPLE

PRESENT	PRESENT
ir	yendo
PAST	**PAST**
haber ido	ido

TENER *to have*

PRESENT	IMPERFECT	FUTURE
1. tengo	tenía	tendré
2. tienes	tenías	tendrás
3. tiene	tenía	tendrá
1. tenemos	teníamos	tendremos
2. tenéis	teníais	tendréis
3. tienen	tenían	tendrán

PRETERITE	PERFECT	PLUPERFECT
1. tuve	he tenido	había tenido
2. tuviste	has tenido	habías tenido
3. tuvo	ha tenido	había tenido
1. tuvimos	hemos tenido	habíamos tenido
2. tuvisteis	habéis tenido	habíais tenido
3. tuvieron	han tenido	habían tenido

PAST ANTERIOR	FUTURE PERFECT
hube tenido *etc*	habré tenido *etc*

CONDITIONAL

IMPERATIVE

PRESENT	PAST	
1. tendría	habría tenido	
2. tendrías	habrías tenido	(tú) **ten**
3. tendría	habría tenido	(Vd) **tenga**
1. tendríamos	habríamos tenido	(nosotros) **tengamos**
2. tendríais	habríais tenido	(vosotros) **tened**
3. tendrían	habrían tenido	(Vds) **tengan**

SUBJUNCTIVE

PRESENT	IMPERFECT	PLUPERFECT
1. tenga	tuv-iera/iese	hubiera tenido
2. tengas	tuv-ieras/ieses	hubieras tenido
3. tenga	tuv-iera/iese	hubiera tenido
1. tengamos	tuv-iéramos/iésemos	hubiéramos tenido
2. tengáis	tuv-ierais/ieseis	hubierais tenido
3. tengan	tuv-ieran/iesen	hubieran tenido

PERFECT
haya tenido *etc*

INFINITIVE

PARTICIPLE

PRESENT	PRESENT
tener	teniendo
PAST	**PAST**
haber tenido	tenido

VENIR *to come*

PRESENT	IMPERFECT	FUTURE
1. vengo	venía	vendré
2. vienes	venías	vendrás
3. viene	venía	vendrá
1. venimos	veníamos	vendremos
2. venís	veníais	vendréis
3. vienen	venían	vendrán

PRETERITE	PERFECT	PLUPERFECT
1. vine	he venido	había venido
2. viniste	has venido	habías venido
3. vino	ha venido	había venido
1. vinimos	hemos venido	habíamos venido
2. vinisteis	habéis venido	habíais venido
3. vinieron	han venido	habían venido

PAST ANTERIOR	FUTURE PERFECT
hube venido *etc*	habré venido *etc*

CONDITIONAL		IMPERATIVE
PRESENT	**PAST**	
1. vendría	habría venido	
2. vendrías	habrías venido	(tú) **ven**
3. vendría	habría venido	(Vd) **veng**a
1. vendríamos	habríamos venido	(nosotros) **veng**amos
2. vendríais	habríais venido	(vosotros) venid
3. vendrían	habrían venido	(Vds) **veng**an

SUBJUNCTIVE

PRESENT	IMPERFECT	PLUPERFECT
1. venga	**vin**-iera/iese	hubiera venido
2. vengas	**vin**-ieras/ieses	hubieras venido
3. venga	**vin**-iera/iese	hubiera venido
1. vengamos	**vin**-iéramos/iésemos	hubiéramos venido
2. vengáis	**vin**-ierais/ieseis	hubierais venido
3. vengan	**vin**-ieran/iesen	hubieran venido

PERFECT
haya venido *etc*

INFINITIVE	PARTICIPLE
PRESENT	**PRESENT**
venir	**vin**iendo
PAST	**PAST**
haber venido	venido

16 VERBS AND THEIR OBJECTS

A number of verbs in Spanish cannot be used without a specific preposition if their object is expressed.

1 Verbs taking a before an object

acercarse a	to approach
aproximarse a	to approach
asistir a	to attend
asomarse a	to lean out of
dar a	to look out onto
faltar a	not to fulfil/keep
jugar a	to play at (*game*)
llegar a	to arrive at/in
oler a	to smell of
oponerse a	to oppose
parecerse a	to resemble
renunciar a	to give up
resistir a	to resist
saber a	to taste of
sobrevivir a	to outlive

faltó a su promesa
he didn't keep his promise

la ventana de mi cuarto daba a un matadero
the window of my room looked out onto an abattoir

la pequeña se parece a su padre
the little girl looks like her father

2 Verbs taking de before an object

abusar de	to misuse
acordarse de	to remember
apoderarse de	to seize
asombrarse de	to wonder at
burlarse de	to make fun of
cambiar de	to change
carecer de	to lack
compadecerse de	to take pity on
depender de	to depend on
desconfiar de	to distrust
despedirse de	to say goodbye to
disfrutar de	to enjoy
dudar de	to doubt
enamorarse de	to fall in love with
enterarse de	to find out
gozar de	to enjoy
maravillarse de	to wonder at
mudar de	to change
ocuparse de	to attend to
olvidarse de	to forget
pasar de	to exceed
prescindir de	to do without
reírse de	to make fun of
responder de	to answer for
saber de	to know of
salir de	to leave (*a place*)
servirse de	to use
sospechar de	to distrust
tirar de	to pull
tratarse de	to be about
variar de	to change
vengarse de	to take revenge for/on

se trata de mi primo
it's about my cousin

afortunadamente gozamos de buena salud
fortunately we enjoy good health

Dudar can be used with the direct object lo in cases like:

lo dudo   **no lo dude Vd.**
I doubt it   don't you doubt it

Otherwise it takes de:

dudo de su testimonio
I doubt his testimony

3 Verbs taking con before an object

acabar con	to put an end to
casarse con	to marry
contar con	to rely on
dar con	to come across
divertirse con	to be amused by
encontrarse con	to meet
hablar con	to talk to
portarse con	to behave towards
soñar con	to dream about

¡acabemos con estas mentiras!
let's put an end to these lies!

cuento contigo
I'm counting on you

4 Verbs taking en before an object

consentir en	to agree to
consistir en	to consist of
convenir en	to agree to
entrar en	to enter/go into

fijarse en	to look at
ingresar en	to enter
penetrar en	to penetrate
pensar en*	to think about
reparar en	to notice

| consintió en ello | ¡fíjate en aquel edificio! |
| he agreed to it | just look at that building! |

*Do not confuse pensar en with pensar de which means 'to have an opinion of':

pensaba en sus vacaciones en España
she was thinking about her holidays in Spain

¿qué piensas de esta idea?
what do you think of this idea?

5 Verbs taking por before an object

asomarse por	to lean out of
felicitar por	to congratulate on
interesarse por	to take an interest in
preguntar por	to ask after

el cura preguntó por mi tía que está enferma
the priest asked after my aunt who is ill

6 Verbs which take no preposition before the object in Spanish though they do in English

agradecer	to be grateful for
aguantar	to put up with
aprobar	to approve of
aprovechar	to take advantage of
buscar	to look for
cuidar	to look after
escuchar	to listen to

esperar	to wait for
extrañar	to wonder at
lamentar	to be sorry about
mirar	to look at
pagar	to pay for
recordar	to remind of
regalar	to make a present of
rumiar	to ponder over
sentir	to be sorry about
soportar	to put up with

aprovecharon la ocasión para felicitar a Juan
they took advantage of the opportunity to congratulate Juan

le agradezco mucho el regalo
thank you very much for the gift

su historia me extraña
your story surprises me

17 VERBS FOLLOWED BY AN INFINITIVE

1 Verbs followed immediately by the infinitive

The direct infinitive is used after the following verbs, though they may also be followed by a clause with its verb in the subjunctive:

a) Verbs of making, advising, ordering, preventing and permitting

aconsejar	to advise to
amenazar	to threaten to
conceder	to concede to
dejar	to let/allow to
hacer	to make
impedir	to prevent from
mandar	to command/order to
ordenar	to command/order to
permitir	to permit/allow to
prohibir	to prohibit from/forbid to

mis padres no me dejan poner la radio después de medianoche
my parents don't allow me to have the radio on after midnight

me mandó salir
he ordered me to leave

b) Verbs of the senses: sentir, ver and oír

oír	to hear
sentir	to feel
ver	to see

no te vi llegar
I didn't see you come in

le oí roncar
I heard him snoring

VERBS FOLLOWED BY AN INFINITIVE

c) Impersonal verbs, where the verb used in the infinitive is the subject of the impersonal verb

alegrarse	**me alegra verte de nuevo** I am happy to see you again
convenir	**no me conviene partir mañana** it doesn't suit me to leave tomorrow
gustar	**nos gusta mucho pasear en el campo** we love walking in the country
hacer falta	**te hace falta estudiar** you need to study
olvidarse	**se me olvidó ir al banco** I forgot to go to the bank
parecer	**¿te parece bien salir ahora?** do you think it's a good idea to leave now?

d) After the following verbs when the subject is the same as that of the infinitive

acordar	to agree to
ansiar	to long to
concertar	to agree to
confesar	to confess to
conseguir	to succeed in -ing, to manage to
creer	to believe
deber	to have to
decidir	to decide to
decir	to say, to tell
descuidar	to neglect to
desear	to wish/want to
esperar	to hope/expect to
evitar	to avoid -ing
figurarse	to suppose, to imagine
fingir	to pretend to
imaginar	to imagine -ing

intentar	to try to
lograr	to succeed in -ing, to manage to
merecer	to merit -ing
necesitar	to need to
negar	to deny -ing
ofrecer	to offer to
olvidar	to forget to
osar	to dare to
parecer	to appear to
pedir	to ask to
pensar	to intend to
poder	to be able to
preferir	to prefer to
presumir	to presume to
pretender	to try/claim to
procurar	to endeavour to
prometer	to promise to
querer	to wish to
recordar	to remember to
resistir	to resist -ing
resolver	to resolve to
resultar	to turn out to (be)
saber	to know how to
sentir	to regret to/-ing
soler	to be accustomed to -ing
temer	to be afraid to

debemos pagar la cuenta ahora
we must pay the bill now

nuestro equipo consiguió ganar el partido
our team managed to win the match

el niño resultó ser el hijo del rey
the boy turned out to be the king's son

solemos merendar en el bosque los domingos
we usually go for a picnic in the woods on Sundays

2 Verbs followed by a + infinitive

The verbs given below take the preposition **a** before a following
infinitive. In most cases the idea of 'in order to' is involved.

a) Verbs of motion

acercarse a	to come forward to
acudir a	to come to
adelantarse a	to go towards
andar a	to go to
apresurarse a	to hurry to
bajar a	to go down to
correr a	to run to
dirigirse a	to go towards ... to
entrar a	to go in to
enviar a	to send to
ir a	to go to
lanzarse a	to rush to
mandar a	to send to
precipitarse a	to rush to
salir a	to go out to
sentarse a	to sit down to
subir a	to go up to
traer a	to bring to
venir a	to come to
volver a	to do ... again

el mecánico se acercó a hablar conmigo
the mechanic came forward to speak to me

la chica se apresuró a hacer las camas
the maid rushed off to make the beds

el jefe mandó al chico a recoger las cartas
the boss sent the boy to pick up the mail

volveré a llamarte mañana
I'll call you again tomorrow

b) Verbs of forcing, compelling, inviting

animar a	to encourage to
conducir a	to lead to
convidar a	to invite to
empujar a	to push into
excitar a	to excite to
exhortar a	to exhort to
forzar a	to force to
impulsar a	to impel to
incitar a	to incite to
inducir a	to induce to
invitar a	to invite to
llamar a	to call to
llevar a	to bring/lead to
obligar a	to oblige to
persuadir a	to persuade to

animaron a la niña a montar al caballo
they encouraged the little girl to get on the horse

el dueño forzó al camarero a limpiar los platos
the owner forced the waiter to clean the plates

me invitó a pasar el fin de semana
he invited me to spend the weekend

c) Verbs of beginning

comenzar a	to begin to
echarse a	to start -ing
empezar a	to begin to
ponerse a	to begin to, to set about -ing
romper a	to break into, to do suddenly

el bebé se echó a llorar
they baby burst into tears

todos los alumnos se pusieron a trabajar
all the pupils started to work

d) Verbs used reflexively to mean deciding or refusing

decidirse a	to decide to
negarse a	to refuse to
resolverse a	to resolve to

el niño se negó a comer
the little boy refused to eat

e) The following verbs

acostumbrarse a	to get used to -ing
aguardar a	to wait to
alcanzar a	to manage to
aprender a	to learn to
arriesgarse a	to risk -ing
aspirar a	to aspire to
atreverse a	to dare to
autorizar a	to authorise to
aventurarse a	to venture to
ayudar a	to help to
comprometerse a	to undertake to
condenar a	to condemn to
contribuir a	to contribute to -ing
dedicarse a	to devote oneself to -ing
detenerse a	to stop to
disponerse a	to get ready to
enseñar a	to teach to
entregarse a	to devote oneself to -ing
exponerse a	to expose oneself to
habituarse a	to get used to -ing
limitarse a	to limit oneself to -ing
ofrecerse a	to offer oneself to
oponerse a	to object to -ing
pararse a	to stop to
prepararse a	to prepare to

quedarse a	to stay and
renunciar a	to give up -ing
resignarse a	to resign oneself to -ing
tender a	to tend to

los chicos no se arriesgaron a cruzar el río
the boys didn't dare cross the river

después del accidente, Juan se dedicó a cuidar de su mujer
after the accident, Juan devoted himself to looking after his wife

se detuvo a hablar conmigo
he stopped to speak to me

3 Verbs followed by de + infinitive

In these cases de is required before a following infinitive:

a) Verbs of stopping or leaving off an action

abstenerse de	to abstain from -ing
acabar de	to finish -ing, to have just
cansarse de	to become tired of -ing
cesar de	to cease -ing
dejar de	to leave off -ing
desistir de	to desist from -ing
disuadir de	to dissuade from -ing
excusar de	to excuse from -ing
fatigarse de	to grow tired of -ing
guardarse de	to take care not to
hartarse de	to grow tired of -ing
librarse de	to escape from -ing
parar de	to stop -ing
saciarse de	to grow tired of -ing
terminar de	to finish -ing

When dejar de is used in the negative, it expresses the idea of 'not to fail to':

no dejes de devolverme los libros la semana que viene
make sure you give me back the books next week

b) Also the following verbs

acordarse de	to remember to
acusar de	to accuse of -ing
alegrarse de	to be glad to
arrepentirse de	to repent of -ing
avergonzarse de	to be ashamed of -ing
consolarse de	to console oneself for -ing
cuidar de	to be careful to
desconfiar de	to mistrust
desesperar de	to despair of -ing
dispensar de	to excuse from -ing
encargarse de	to undertake to, to see to -ing
jactarse de	to boast of -ing
maravillarse de	to marvel at
olvidarse de	to forget to
no poder por menos de	not to be able to help -ing
tratar de	to try to
tratarse de	to be a question of

yo me encargo de hacer eso
I'll see to doing that

el joven se olvidó de acudir a la cita
the young man forgot to keep his appointment

se trata de trabajar más
it's a question of working more

no pude por menos de reírme
I couldn't help laughing

4 Verbs followed by en + infinitive

complacerse en	to take pleasure in -ing
consentir en	to consent to
consistir en	to consist in -ing
convenir en	to agree to

dudar en	to hesitate to
empeñarse en	to insist on -ing
entretenerse en	to amuse oneself in -ing
esforzarse en	to try hard to
hacer bien en	to do well/right to
hacer mal en	to do badly/wrong in
insistir en	to insist on -ing
interesarse en	to be interested in -ing
obstinarse en	to be determined to
pensar en	to think of -ing
persistir en	to persist in -ing
quedar en	to agree to
soñar en	to have in mind to
tardar en	to take (a long) time to
vacilar en	to hesitate to

la niña se esforzaba en montar en bicicleta
the little girl was trying hard to ride the bicycle

haces bien en aydar a tu madre
you do well to help your mother

los amigos quedaron en verse a los ocho
the friends agreed to meet at eight o'clock

el tren tardó treinta minutos en llegar
the train took thirty minutes to come

5 Verbs followed by con + infinitive

amenazar con	to threaten to
contentarse con	to content oneself with -ing
soñar con	to dream of -ing

el hombre de negocios soñaba con ir a Río de Janeiro
the business man dreamed of going off to Rio

VERBS FOLLOWED BY AN INFINITIVE

6 Verbs followed by por + infinitive

a) Verbs of beginning and ending, with the sense of English 'by'

acabar por	to end up by -ing
comenzar por	to begin by -ing
empezar por	to begin by -ing

acabó por comprarse el traje azul
she finished up buying the blue suit

b) Verbs of longing/trying to *etc*

esforzarse por	to make an effort to
luchar por	to struggle to
morirse por	to be dying to
rabiar por	to be dying to

la niña se moría por abrir los paquetes
the little girl was dying to open the parcels

18 Conjunctions

1 Simple conjunctions

Simple conjunctions consist of one word only. The commonest are:

aunque	although
como	as *(reason)*
conforme	as *(in proportion as)*
conque	so, so then
cuando	when
e	and
mas*	but
mientras	while
ni	neither/nor
o	or
pero	but
porque	because
pues	since, so
que	that, for *(because)*
según	according to
si	if, whether
sino	but
siquiera	if only
u	or
y	and

* Mas is old-fashioned nowadays, the everyday word for 'but' being pero.

> **me fui al cine porque creía que ya no venías**
> I went to the cinema because I thought you weren't coming

> **sabremos pronto si hemos ganado el premio**
> we'll soon know whether we've won the prize

> **se puso triste cuando se murió su perro**
> he became sad when his dog died

> **no grites tanto, que ya te oigo**
> don't shout so much, I can hear you

2 Compound conjunctions

These conjunctions consist of two or more words, the last one usually being que:

a condición de que	on condition that
a fin de que	so that
a medida que	as
a menos que	unless
a no ser que	unless
antes de que	before
a pesar de que	despite
así que	so (that)
con tal (de) que	provided that
de manera que	so (that)
de modo que	so (that)
desde que	since
después de que	after
en caso de que	in case
hasta que	until
luego que	as soon as
mientras	while
mientras que	whereas
para que	in order that
por lo que	for which reason
por si	in case
puesto que	since (reason)
salvo que	except that
siempre que	whenever, so long as
sino que	but
tan pronto como	as soon as
ya que	since (reason)

vamos a preparar la comida por si vienen pronto
let's get the meal ready in case they come soon

los niños jugaban mientras su madre se ocupaba de la casa
the children played while their mother took care of the house

llevo el paraguas por si llueve
I'll take my umbrella in case it rains

Note

Whereas **puesto que** and **ya que** refer to cause, **desde que** refers only to time in Spanish:

todo marcha bien desde que él llegó
everything has been fine since he arrived

puesto que las mercancías ya no están disponibles
since the goods are no longer available

3 Coordinating conjunctions

Coordinating conjunctions come in pairs and are used to link two closely associated ideas:

apenas ... (cuando)	hardly ... when
bien ... bien	either ... or
ni ... ni	neither ... nor
no ... sino	not ... but
no ... pero sí	not ... but
no sólo ... sino también	not only ... but also
o ... o	either ... or
o bien ... o bien	either ... or
que ... o que	whether ... or
tanto ... como	both ... and
ya ... ya	sometimes ... sometimes

ni los sindicatos ni los empresarios están contentos
neither the unions nor the employers are happy

tanto tú como yo
both you and I

19 NUMBERS

1 The cardinal numbers

0	cero	10	diez
1	uno, una	11	once
2	dos	12	doce
3	tres	13	trece
4	cuatro	14	catorce
5	cinco	15	quince
6	seis	16	dieciséis
7	siete	17	diecisiete
8	ocho	18	dieciocho
9	nueve	19	diecinueve

20	veinte	21	veintiuno
22	veintidós	23	veintitrés
24	veinticuatro	25	veinticinco
26	veintiséis	27	veintisiete
28	veintiocho	29	veintinueve

30	treinta	31	treinta y uno/una
40	cuarenta	42	cuarenta y dos
50	cincuenta	53	cincuenta y tres
60	sesenta	64	sesenta y cuatro
70	setenta	75	setenta y cinco
80	ochenta	86	ochenta y seis
90	noventa	97	noventa y siete

100	ciento	101	ciento uno/una
105	ciento cinco	115	ciento quince
120	ciento veinte	123	ciento veintitrés
150	ciento cincuenta	176	ciento setenta y seis

200	doscientos/as	202	doscientos dos
300	trescientos/as	317	trescientos diecisiete
400	cuatrocientos/as	428	cuatrocientos veintiocho
500	quinientos/as	539	quinientos treinta y nueve
600	seiscientos/as	645	seiscientos cuarenta y cinco
700	setecientos/as	754	setecientos cincuenta y cuatro
800	ochocientos/as	863	ochocientos sesenta y tres
900	novecientos/as	971	novecientos setenta y uno/una

1,000	mil	2,000	dos mil
3,000	tres mil	4,000	cuatro mil
5,000	cinco mil	6,000	seis mil
7,000	siete mil	8,000	ocho mil
9,000	nueve mil	10,000	diez mil

200,000	doscientos mil
300,000	trescientos mil
600,000	seiscientos mil
1,000,000	un millón
2,000,000	dos millones

a) Alternative forms

There are alternative forms for 16 to 19 which are written as three separate words:

diez y seis, diez y siete *etc*

b) Shortened forms of certain numbers

Uno is shortened to un when followed by a noun or adjective + noun:

treinta y un meses
thirty-one months

doscientos un días
two hundred and one days

Ciento is shortened to cien when followed by (1) a noun, (2) an adjective + noun, (3) the numerals mil and millones:

cien panes	**cien mil hojas**
a hundred loaves	a hundred thousand leaves
cien buenos días	**cien millones de euros**
a hundred good days	a hundred million euros

c) Agreement

Cardinal numbers are invariable except for the plural hundreds and numbers ending in -uno:

doscientas personas	**quinientas cincuenta libras**
two hundred people	five hundred and fifty pounds
veintiuna páginas	**ciento una cosas**
twenty-one pages	a hundred and one things

d) Accents

Written accents are necessary for some of the twenties:

22 **veintidós**, 23 **veintitrés**, 26 **veintiséis**

also: **veintiún años**
        twenty-one years

e) Counting by hundreds stops at 900

1966	**mil novecientos sesenta y seis**
	nineteen hundred and sixty-six
1200 euros	**mil doscientos euros**
	twelve hundred euros

2 The ordinal numbers

primero	first	**sexto**	sixth
segundo	second	**séptimo**	seventh
tercero	third	**octavo**	eighth
cuarto	fourth	**noveno**	ninth
quinto	fifth	**décimo**	tenth

a) Ordinals are adjectives and as such agree with their noun:

    la segunda esquina   **la séptima semana**
    the second corner   the seventh week

b) Primero and tercero are shortened to primer and tercer before a
    masculine singular noun:

    el primer tren   **el tercer coche**
    the first train   the third coach

c) Ordinals are rarely used beyond the tenth, when cardinals are
    used instead:

    el siglo once   **Luis XIV – Luis catorce**
    the eleventh century   Louis the fourteenth

20 DAYS, MONTHS AND SEASONS

The names of the days of the week, the months and the seasons are written with small letters in Spanish.

a) Days of the week

el lunes	Monday
el martes	Tuesday
el miércoles	Wednesday
el jueves	Thursday
el viernes	Friday
el sábado	Saturday
el domingo	Sunday

b) Months

enero	January
febrero	February
marzo	March
abril	April
mayo	May
junio	June
julio	July
agosto	August
se(p)tiembre	September
octubre	October
noviembre	November
diciembre	December

c) Seasons

primavera	spring
verano	summer
otoño	autumn
invierno	winter

INDEX